REDISCOVER YOUR LOVE LIFE

YOGI SHASHI PENUMARTHY

CONTENTS

PREFACE

WHY WRITE THIS BOOK?

This book is the culmination of 42 years of work, both spiritual and worldly, during which I engaged with thousands of people and many spiritual entities in order to discover, learn, understand and communicate insights, wisdom and love for the benefit of humanity.

For the first 33 years of my life, I was in total surrender to the Divine Feminine, the highest feminine intelligence in existence and beyond. She is also the ultimate manifestation of the one power from which all else flows. During those years, my life was completely under the control of her Grace and there was little I could do beyond witnessing my life unfolding in front of me at light speed. I watched my body move in the world, speak, write, engage and perform all kinds of functions that are normal to an Earthly existence, without having any say in the matter. On the inside, my world was completely still and silent. I had no thoughts and no feelings—only sensations that I later understood to be bursts of energy leaving my body, leaving me weak and vulnerable to disease as time went on.

During this time, I experienced a great deal of suffering, due entirely to other people (mostly women), who constantly took what they needed from me (mostly my energy) and did little or nothing to help me sustain myself in order that I may continue my work. But what was my work anyway?

The Divine Feminine put me through a whole lifetime of experiences in a very short amount of time, which included growing up, moving to the United States, earning an advanced degree and finding a job. While on the outside my life was seemingly quite ordinary, on the inside, a whole slew of spiritual experiences was being given to me and soon after became conscious. All of these experiences involved the feminine in some form or another and I found myself being given to the women of the world as a source of energy regardless of who they were, what they wanted and how they treated me. The women to whom I gave my energy were almost always abusive, at least at the level of energy where I was focused, but the point of these experiences was not to simply abuse me. As these women received my energy, they gave me access to their inner world and I saw exactly how they lived spiritually and energetically. As a direct consequence, this also revealed to me how the world actually works at the level of energies, as opposed to how people believe it works.

The vast majority of human beings on this Earth live in spiritual darkness. They have little happiness, no ecstasy and not even any deep insight into the way life is going, other than whatever they may have encountered and memorized by reading scripture or listening to some holy men. This is much more so the case with women, who have essentially been forgotten by the world and are being treated as props, toys, or worse, used and squeezed out of all their vital energies for the entertainment, pleasure or comfort of others. The inner world of most women, much of which is invisible to women themselves, was exposed to me, showing me the level of corruption and decrepitude that had entered their bodies over millennia, due mainly to a total neglect of their spiritual development.

Unfortunately, most of the oppression that women endure is due either to themselves, or to other women, but this is something women neither know, nor understand deeply. And consequently, they do not know how to free themselves from this oppression, which has now become systematized and acceptable in the form of the many rules, regulations and limitations placed upon humanity in general. The consequences of such oppression have spilled over into the lives of the boys as well, most of whom no longer have mothers that can teach them how to be, how to live and how to love. Boys learn only from their mothers—in fact, they see all women as their mother—and for a very long time, boys have not received the kind of instruction they need to become good human beings. These boys then grow up physically, but not spiritually and become horrible fathers and partners, easily swayed by the temptations and distractions of the world, further contributing to the corruption of young people by their actions and their example.

The reality of the energy system of males and females is that it is a *lot* easier to eliminate the corruption in a male than it is in a female because the male is simpler in many ways. Despite this, and the fact that the vast majority of spiritual practices that have been given to humanity are aimed at the boys, the boys on this planet have not done the right thing. The males on this planet, in general, have not done the necessary spiritual work despite having every opportunity to do so.

The consequence of all this is that after many thousands of years of human civilization, society is at its worst, not just spiritually, but emotionally and even materially, while it continues to measure progress in terms of comfort, convenience and access to pleasure. Inequality has become the norm, not the exception. Racism is accepted as something that just happens to be around, not an abhorrent outlier in human experience. Misogyny is not just alive but is being actively supported. And young men are nowhere to be found, mostly having been enslaved by the system and turned into robots simply carrying out their masters' instructions.

The roots of this corruption do not lie in capitalism, politics, the education system, religion, spirituality or even human nature. The roots of all these ills plaguing humanity lie in something much simpler: the lack of understanding as to why we are here, what we are here to do and how we are supposed to live.

While many religious books, scriptures and spiritual writings have come and gone, humanity has not received a simple, step-by-step guide addressing the many areas of life that need to be paid attention to, and more importantly, *the way* they need to be paid attention to for life to go well. Undue amounts of emphasis have been placed on things such as worldly success or inner peace and many yogic techniques have been introduced among the populace in hopes of moving things forward, but this is not what you, the young people of the world, have ever needed. While our young people continue to struggle to manage basic things (such as their feelings), just about everyone who has an opinion has decided to share whatever they believe can lead to material success or spiritual enlightenment. Self-help gurus constantly tout the benefits of the right attitude, or "qualities" such as determination and persistence, while holy men have continued to share chants, prayers, mantras, tantras, meditations, kriyas—you name it. And finally, religious leaders have of course always tried to communicate only one idea: that one must have *faith* in a higher power and surrender, but even they fall short of showing young people *how* they can surrender.

And in any case, when was the last time you heard anyone provide any proof that God, or a higher power exists and is actively guiding the lives of people on this Earth? Such talk usually rests on assuming that you can point to something and say 'Look, there it is!' and hope that the other person can see what you're pointing at. But if the other person's vision is unclear to begin with, what do you expect them to see?

What young people like you need is a path you can follow that, first and foremost, guides you on how you can live such that your own vision is clarified. Second, once you begin to see clearly, you need help with staying on track and not losing your clarity while the world continues to conjure up new ways of distracting and derailing your lives. Third, you need guidance on how to *love* in a way that enriches, enlivens and enlightens. These three steps are designed to do one thing and only one thing: to raise your intelligence so you can handle your life with ease, find answers to your own questions and live a beautiful life, while creating a better world along the way.

This book will address the first two steps, while Volume III will address the topics of love, sex and relationships, which require far more spiritual maturity to put in practice harmoniously than most people realize that they do.

In these books, I will address every single major question that you are struggling with: questions of identity, gender, money and power, wealth and influence, success and failure, relationships, how the world works, religion, spiritual practice, even the role of death and dissolution. If you follow the path laid out in this book to the best of your ability (and survive!), you will understand the meaning of your own life without any doubt and be well on your way to total spiritual enlightenment.

WHY FOCUS ONLY ON YOUNG PEOPLE?

After 33 years of spiritual surrender, I went through a 7-year period of healing and recovery. During these 7 years, I was married, had a child, went through a divorce and was transformed into someone who could communicate these insights to you. The Divine Feminine and I spent those 7 years revisiting my life experiences, making conscious spiritual experiences, crystallizing these experiences into narratives, then refining, writing, speaking, sharing and re-refining these narratives until they became accessible to normal people on this Earth. Accordingly, I do not use any spiritually-charged terminology because it is of no use to someone who hasn't experienced anything spiritual in the first place. Nor do I engage in metaphysical poetry and descriptions of "the world beyond" in order to communicate something ineffable. My goal is simple: to give you, the young person reading this book, practical guidance to help you live a beautiful life and create a better world along the way.

But there is a catch: you must have energy.

We, the Yogis of the world, have always been interested only in the young, because we know for a fact that no one else will succeed in becoming enlightened in a single lifetime. Spirituality isn't for the weak or for those who aren't willing to develop the courage needed to live a full life. You will not have the wisdom, the fortitude and strength to withstand all of life's vicissitudes on day one, but you must have the willingness and the commitment to follow through with whatever it is you have decided to try in your own life. It is not important that you succeed on the first try either. All you need is to keep trying, at your own pace. And this takes enormous amounts of energy; energy only the young people on this Earth have.

But how do I define young?

A young person is anyone who has enough energy left to complete their journey to spiritual enlightenment and create a beautiful life for themselves. It is not important that you succeed on this journey in this lifetime, only that you have enough energy to begin. Why this is the case will become clear as you read this book.

During my travels across the United States, I observed a pattern that allows me to express this prerequisite in terms of age and gender. A young woman, i.e., a female with an exceptional level of femininity, is ripe for beginning her spiritual practice around 17 years old. A young man, i.e., a male with an exceptional level of masculinity, is ready around 12 years old. The level of energy available to human beings drops off quickly with age, and by the time either gender has reached around 50 years old, there is not much hope left, although I have encountered some great exceptions myself. My books aren't written for children though. In fact, all my writings are for mature adults who can decide for themselves what is best for them. If you are an enlightened parent, you are welcome to guide your child on the path of light using this book if you choose.

The difference between genders has nothing to do with physiology and everything to do with the level of masculinity or femininity in the energies of the individual. Accordingly, those who consider themselves transgender or gender-fluid will have to experiment in order to understand where they fall on the spectrum between masculinity and femininity and adjust their lifestyles accordingly.

Regardless, no matter how the world sees you, or how you see yourself today, understand this: if you have the energy to succeed, success will not be denied to you. That is my promise.

HOW TO USE THIS BOOK

You must read this book from cover to cover, in sequence. Do not skip chapters or sections that don't make sense. Sometimes, you will need a higher level of intelligence than you have been operating with for a section to make sense. In such cases, you must be willing to wait for your intelligence to rise and for that section to make sense before you move on. Your subconscious will do the wondering, pondering, analyses, etc. on your behalf, so you don't have to sit around thinking about a section if you don't want to. But you must not rush through this book hoping to make sense of it on the first try. It will not.

You must be willing to take the time and go through this book slowly. I have written this book so as to be a lifelong companion for most of you, because that's how long it will take for most of you to succeed. Do not worry about losing steam along the way if it takes you a few decades to make it. If you start young, as long as you follow the guidance in this book, you will have the energy you need to keep going all lifelong.

This book is not entertainment, nor is it a self-help book. I am actually not going to give you many details on how to live, but I will spend a lot of time discussing the principles so that you may put them into practice in a way that makes sense for you. This book is a serious spiritual guide that will affect profound changes to your life *and to your world.*

Do not take that last sentence lightly. The power that I will help you develop will literally change your body and the physical reality around you. If you are unhealthy, you will be free of disease. If you carry too much weight, it will disappear. If you have toxic people around you, they will vanish and be replaced with loving human beings. All that is wrong for you will simply dissolve into nothingness and only that which is right for you will remain in your world. Material prosperity is not guaranteed, because material prosperity is completely valueless and useless for living a beautiful life. What you need is *actual wealth,* meaning you will have enough to live and to do what you really want to do. And that is enough.

But in order to succeed, you must give it your all. If your focus is on something else other than your life, you will fail. Your home, your career, your clothing, your lifestyle, your relationships, etc. are accessories, not your life itself, and everything that isn't your life, *in essence,* will be considered fair game for remodeling, so to speak. You must be willing to leave behind all that is bad for you and accept radical changes when they happen, because once your inner intelligence starts to function on your behalf, it will not stop and ask you for your opinion. It will forge ahead at light speed and you will have to keep up. Think of it as traveling in a rocket ship—you will not have time to look out the window and admire the scenery flashing by at a million miles an hour.

Which brings me to the most important warning I have for all young people who wish to change their lives: this book and any further volumes I write are a form of Yoga. No, they are not the kind of Yoga where you strike a pose, but they are a form of Yoga nonetheless. All forms of Yoga are extremely potent, powerful and inherently dangerous. Every form of Yoga is designed to essentially reshape your world and they do so by first destroying the world in which you live today. This means that, like all forms of Yoga, neither success nor survival is guaranteed on the path of light laid out in this book because most people run out of energy before the end and perish. Yogis like me have made it all the way because we have lived fearlessly, not squandered even an iota of energy on things that don't matter *and* not cared about persecution, destitution, dismemberment or death. When it comes to Yoga, you will succeed only if you are willing to put everything on the line. Even then, for some people that success may come only at the moment of their death.

Young men will find all the guidance they need in these volumes, because the path for a young man is much simpler than that for a young woman. Young women will need a little bit more understanding, but there are some things about feminine power I am not allowed to reveal in a publicly-accessible volume. Young women who still have questions after finishing this book are welcome to come to me, preferably in groups.

All my love and the Grace of the Divine Feminine are available to you, if you allow it to come into your life. Thank you for taking the first step to becoming a free, fully-fledged human being.

—Shashi Penumarthy
November 14, 2023
Tucson, AZ

VOLUME I

THE CHOICE

THE PATH OF DARKNESS

The *need to believe* is something that people have been holding onto for so long that it has become a religion unto itself. There is no shortage of celebrities, self-help gurus, billboards, music, movies, corporations and religious institutions that all want you to believe in something, even if only in yourself. The near-constant brainwashing in American society from entities that want you to believe in one thing or another has taken its toll on the populace: at this point, most people don't know what to believe anymore.

Should you believe in Jesus? Or God, maybe? Should you believe your president? Perhaps you believe that your parents are good people and worth believing. Maybe you are sold on the economic system and totally believe in the power of the market, or the power of money. Maybe you are agnostic and don't believe in a higher power at the moment, or you are given over to science and are convinced that sooner or later we will have enough knowledge to understand it all. Or perhaps you like superhero movies and are convinced that all you have to do is believe in yourself.

But let me ask you something: have you experienced any of the things that you have been asked to believe in? Have you experienced Jesus, or God? Mind you, experience is a very high bar in human life. You must not call something an experience if you cannot be totally sure it happened. If you get soaked in a rainstorm, for example, you will not have to believe that it happened. If you eat an ice cream and feel amazing, you will not have to believe that you had an ice cream. If you experience the sun shining, you don't have to analyze, think about and try to convince yourself that the sun is, in fact, shining. That's what I am calling *experience*. It is something you had that is unambiguous, undeniable and beyond any doubt.

So, have you experienced anything you have been asked to believe in? Are you really convinced that the market economy works for the benefit of all, for example? Has your own life experience convinced you beyond a shadow of doubt that money is power? Are you convinced that having many followers on social media will help you in your life? Do you believe in yourself (whatever that means)?

If you are, in fact, convinced that you should believe in any of the things that you have heard about, felt or maybe seen, then you really should go full tilt, pursue whatever it is you believe in, and fail. It is the surest and fastest way to enlightenment, by far. I am not joking with you. All yogis have always encouraged those who want to go down a certain path to go down that path with whatever they have and to put all their energies, resources, time—everything—into it, and fail. A spectacular failure like that is a surefire way to become instantly enlightened and live a life of peace, serenity, beauty and happiness, because what it does is destroy *all* of your false beliefs in one fell swoop and firmly grounds you in reality.

But why would you fail? You would fail because if something were real, like sunshine, you wouldn't have to believe in it. You would just know. The very act of believing implies that you don't know that it is real. Believing is *gambling*. It is a way of saying 'I don't know but at some point, I hope it reveals itself to be what I believe it to be'.

Now, here's how the world works when it comes to gambling. You need a lot of people to put their time, attention, energy—whatever they have—into something they believe in, in the hopes that at some point, at least one of them will score the ultimate prize associated with that belief, whatever it may be. After all, all beliefs come with the promise of some great reward. In other words, a belief that comes with a big reward is a shared delusion and the larger the number of people who share that belief, the bigger the prize.

So, if you believe in something, and you want to succeed in the world, what you have to do is convince many others to believe in that same thing, while ensuring that none of them will win the ultimate prize. Casinos are masters at this game, as are many financial firms, business people and so on. In fact, almost everyone you see in the world that has a lot of wealth is a master at this game: convincing enough people to believe in something while ensuring that none of them will win. Sure, the people who believe may get a little bit of a reward here and there, but they will never have it all. Politicians have recently understood this game a bit better than they used to and so they are doing their level best to try and align themselves with the right set of beliefs, one that will get them the maximum amount of attention, energy and time from the people who they depend on for their livelihood. So are news organizations, charities, environmental associations and even individuals on social media.

But haven't some of these people succeeded in the world? Yes, they have, to some extent, but *you* will fail, simply because you picked up this book.

See, the problem with most people who wish—at some level—to succeed in the world, is that they are hoping to do it the *nice* way, the *good* way, the *moral* way, the *ethical* way. Most people, unfortunately, are interested in making *an honest living*, as they put it. And this is a surefire way to fail, because you cannot be *good* and simultaneously play the game where you succeed by making others believe in a delusion. If you want to succeed in the world, you must play the game and play it ruthlessly. You must be willing to defeat everyone else, at any cost. You must be predatory, manipulative, devious, unethical, immoral and willing to act as if you are above the law. It is extremely important that you do this, or you will fail. It doesn't really matter that you, too, are caught up in the delusion—that you, too, believe in what you are asking others to believe in. As long as you ensure that no one else can win, you will succeed.

Understand that when I talk about worldly success, I am not talking about little accomplishments like winning the gold medal at the Olympics.

Little things like that can happen even if you live an impeccably honest life, although they are becoming less likely as the world becomes more focused on performance and less on actual skill and ability. Still, however great such things might seem, they are tiny compared to the world and its possibilities. Success means that you have it all, and *worldly* success means that you literally have everything that is possible to buy in this world. This definition works because success in *life*, i.e., spiritual success, does in fact mean that you will have all the good things that life has to offer: generosity, sweetness, kindness, wisdom, happiness, peace, love—you name it. In fact, you will have more of all the good stuff than you will know what to do with.

So, if you want worldly success, you will have to deny, reject and give up all that you know is good. There is no place in life for the good things to co-exist with worldly success. Sure, when you are successful in the world, you will have lots of people around you telling you that you have all the good things in life, but you will know, in your own heart, that you don't.

If you picked up my book, it is only because at some level, you are interested in goodness, kindness, sweetness, happiness, love and so on. If this is the kind of human being you are, you are incapable of the ruthlessness that it takes to succeed in the world. In other words, metaphorically speaking, you are interested in living in light, not in darkness.

But since the only way to succeed in the world is to walk the path of darkness, most people choose the dark path, while simultaneously telling themselves that they believe in goodness, kindness, happiness and so on. As a result, most people live mediocre lives succeeding neither in the world, nor in life. They have little material wealth, not much money, absolutely no love to share, zero wisdom, and they live meaningless lives that are totally dependent on having lots of support mechanisms to make them feel better—everything from caffeine and alcohol, friends and social networks, to social security and benefits. And of course, the path of darkness leads to a bitter, unfulfilled end, even if you have a few accomplishments along the way, even if you have a few moments of peace and happiness. That, in a nutshell, is the fate awaiting the vast majority of human beings.

So, the first lesson for you is this: if you want to succeed in the world, walk the path of darkness wholeheartedly. Stop reading this book. Take up whatever suggestion the world is giving you, whether that be to build followers, sell yourself or your skills in some way, work hard and make lots of money, acquire connections and power, etc., because the world is right—those *are*, in fact, all the things that you will need in order to succeed in the world, no question. And if you do decide to walk that path, do it fervently, vigorously and ruthlessly. Let the world see a person that is so unbelievably focused on worldly success that it bows down to you. That is the way.

You will not understand this right now, but the ultimate power in the universe will be your ally even if you decide to walk the path of darkness. Do not think that you will not be empowered if you make this choice. The powers that be will, in fact, push you down your chosen path as quickly as possible. This has always been true.

I am telling you all this because now more than ever, we need our young people to commit, either to go down the path of light, or the path of darkness. It is this lack of commitment and decisiveness that is causing so many young people to feel like life has no direction, no meaning, and so on. It is causing many young people to think about committing suicide, into becoming addicted or falling prey to the wrong sort of influences on social media. There is no sense in dilly-dallying, being indecisive and hoping that someday you will find a middle way where both spiritual and material success can be found. There is no middle way. You must choose.

Unless, you want to remain skeptical and be open to the path of light revealing itself to you.

THE SKEPTIC

Being skeptical is very different from believing in something or not believing in something. Being skeptical means that you are open, that you have not made up your mind. It means, for example, that you have not yet decided that you want worldly success at the cost of your own happiness, well-being and love.

If you are, in fact, skeptical, life will repeatedly give you experiences that will force you to choose. Every interaction, every moment, every action will be full of choices, choices that will force you to decide who you are. Every choice will build upon the choices you made before, avalanching you down either the path of light or the path of darkness. Pretty soon, these choices will become automatic and you will hurtle down your chosen path at full speed and arrive at the end. You will finish before this lifetime ends. Enlightenment will be yours, *no matter what your path ultimately looks like.*

But being a skeptic is very, very hard. Wherever you go, people and situations will force you to commit to a belief system of some sort. If you go to school, you will be confronted with a system of beliefs that you will have to reject. If you go to work, you will be confronted with a different set of beliefs that you will have to reject as well. This will happen to you at home, in church, at the park, on your football team, at the grocery store, even in a national park. If you are truly a skeptic, every single belief, however well supported by arguments, will grate on you. You will have to live a life where you don't believe a thing, and consequently, don't *know* a thing. If you question the people that share knowledge as to how they know something, you will soon realize that all knowledge is based on belief and feel even more ignorant.

If you are truly skeptical, a day will come when you look at the body and wonder 'what is this?' or 'who am I?' And you will need to live in that state of total ignorance for a long time before you will find an answer. Meanwhile, the world in which we live, which is almost entirely based on knowledge at this point, will constantly subject you to ridicule and torture. You will be ostracized, cast out and have to wander around trying to fit in, fruitlessly, for in general, people are more than willing to simply accept whatever they are asked to believe in for the sake of survival. And you will be seen as a threat to it all.

There is a name for this path, you know: Jnana Yoga, the path of inquiry. And it is the hardest path of all. I don't want you to follow this path, because almost none of you will survive if you do. And I am not here to help the skeptics.

DECISION TIME

What is the path of light then? The rest of this volume and the volumes to come. But before you decide to continue reading further, you must make a choice:

Do you want happiness, love and all the good stuff that comes with it, which includes a beautiful life, a peaceful world, sweet relationships, independence, lots of energy and boundless wisdom to share? If so, continue reading this book.

Do you want worldly success, material prosperity, fame and fortune, lots of pleasures, comforts and sex, the adulation of many, dependency on many supports without which you cannot survive, and a bad end, even though you will have lots of "fun" along the way? If so, drop this book and continue living however you want to live.

LOVE

THE WHOLE SHEBANG

On a beautiful fall morning in Apex, North Carolina, towards the end of my 7-year healing period, I was sitting in the house that my wife at the time and I were living in, ready to start my daily spiritual practice. The last 7 years of healing had taken an enormous toll on my physical body. I had gained a lot of weight and was also generally very weak, as all of my energy was being spent on healing the deeper layers in my body, and very little energy was available for my physical body to stay in good health.

Now I am not the kind of yogi that has been blessed with solitude in the world or a life where I live in seclusion in the Himalayas, an Ashram or a yoga center of sorts. I have been a yogi that has lived in, and worked in, the world that all of us share and know. I have been through the education system that many have, earned a Bachelor's and a Master's degree, and held many jobs. Even today, I do my own taxes, buy my own groceries, cook my own food, do my own laundry—you get the idea. I have not been isolated from the world, nor insulated from all its pain and suffering. In fact, I have had a front-row seat to the hidden suffering among human beings, thanks to a deeper yogic vision I was given that allowed me to see into the energy system of people and understand just how much sadness and anger there was within, not to mention a million other issues, such as insecurities, pain, trauma, influences from past lives and so on.

You do not have to believe me when I talk about things that sound "supernatural," but do not simply dismiss my life experience either, for if you do, you will do the same to your own life experience and soon become very disillusioned with all of life. Respect the fact that human beings are extremely varied and capable in many ways that you may not yet understand and be open to the fact that others may have had an experience that you haven't had. The guidance I provide in this book doesn't require you to believe what I am saying about how I learned what I did, but it does require that you keenly observe your own life experience and learn from it. And there is no way you will be able to make sense of your own life if you dismiss some of your experiences as being "random" or "not important," while focusing only on experiences the world thinks are worth something. You must pay attention to every single moment of your life in order to make sense of it.

And so it was that in addition to my spiritual work, I was also fulfilling many worldly responsibilities. We had a child in the home that needed caring for. I had a job as a Product Manager for a pretty reputable company in Raleigh, and my wife had decided to buy a big house with lots of space that also took a fair amount of maintenance and upkeep. On top of all this, I was the one in the home that did most of the cooking. These responsibilities and duties would leave me totally exhausted by the end of each day and the lack of energy meant that I would have trouble falling asleep. It's like being wound up all the time—you can't relax.

Thankfully, just when I needed support, a guru had come into my life (uninvited!) and shared with me a Kriya (a kind of exercise) that would raise my energy, allow me to continue to heal, live my life, as well as endure the many spiritual experiences that were coming and going during those days without falling apart. I will say more about this guru later, but this is something gurus often do—they simply walk into the lives of people who need them. I trusted this guru and my commitment to the guru's instructions was absolute and unwavering.

I would wake up every morning, take a shower and do my Kriya exactly as the guru instructed. At the end of the Kriya, I would experience a surge of energy and a few hours later, a soft feeling of bliss would pervade my whole world. I would end up flying through my work day with little to no pain, as if I had been given a potent mix of caffeine and opium. However, once I got home, the effects of the Kriya would start to wear off, and by the time I got into bed, they would disappear, leaving me totally spent and in severe pain once again.

As it happened though, on this particular morning, as I finished my Kriya, I noticed that my energy, which usually rose to a certain point and held, was rising and rising and kept going up and up, until I nearly lost all consciousness.

Now, I was ready to die during this Kriya—I've always known that death is a myth so I've never been afraid of it—but I wasn't exactly expecting to go so suddenly, especially with a wife and child in the home. Still, as I started to feel like I might lose consciousness, I gave in as I always did, and with my eyes closed, arrived in a space that was utterly still, dark and silent.

Now there is something you need to understand about all spiritual experience: it is not an "escape" from physical reality. Spiritual experiences always involve experiencing *additional* dimensions other than the physical dimension we are all used to experiencing. You don't lose total consciousness, nor do you lose total awareness of your surroundings. It's as if in addition to this world, another world comes into your experience. This isn't that different from what you experience when you have a strong feeling—it may take over for a bit, but you don't totally lose awareness of what's going on around you. The difference, though, is that spiritual experiences are completely non-sensory in nature (but not nonsensical!). They don't unfold in the realm of sight, sound, taste, touch and smell. However, since the English language does not have vocabulary suited to describing spiritual dimensions, we end up using terminology that is commonly applied to physical reality.

So, when I describe a spiritual experience and I say that "I saw," I am not saying that I saw in the same way I would see a phone sitting next to me. However, the experience of "seeing," "hearing," etc. during a spiritual experience is no less real. In fact, in most cases, it is more real in a way that will not make sense to you unless you've actually had a spiritual experience yourself.

As I sat in total silence, I distinctly remember the neighbor's dog barking outside, and I remember being aware of the light from my neighbor's porch streaming through the blinds in the room I was sitting in. But soon, my focus shifted inward and the darkness within me started to give way to a scene that I can only describe as ethereal.

In a vast dark space, the expanse of which seemed totally unfathomable, I saw at a very far distance a few "clouds." Each of these clouds was illuminated by some kind of light, but the light was not coming from within the clouds. It was clear that there was some kind of invisible light pervading the sky of darkness and that this light became apparent only due to contact with the clouds I was seeing.

As I looked, spellbound, everything became clear to me in a flash. I *knew*, instantly, that the clouds I was looking at were clouds of consciousness, that each cloud of consciousness contained one existence each, and that each existence contained multiple universes. I remember distinctly *knowing* which of those clouds we live in—i.e., which one our universe was located in—while being simultaneously flabbergasted at just how many existences and universes there were.

We are not alone, not by a long shot!

As I "stared" with my eyes closed, my focus shifted away from the clouds to the light. I saw that this light was coming from behind me and that it was everywhere. And again, in a flash, it became clear to me what I was looking at.

The darkness pervading all, is what we call *awareness*, the clouds are what we call *consciousness*, and the light is what we know as love. These things were not abstract concepts, but simply different levels of intelligence and energy, and I perceived them as clearly as one perceives daylight.

I am not trying to tell you that what I saw was a metaphorical image of some sort or a hallucination. I am telling you that this is how existence is made. This is what it actually looks like once you step outside the bounds of human experience, step back as far as you can, and look at life from the outside, so to speak. If you had an experience that showed you how all of life was put together—and I have had many, many experiences, some of which I will share in this book—you would be instantly free of all fear, confusion, darkness, anxiety, depression, illness—indeed all negativity. Once you've had such an experience, it would take a while for this freedom and fearlessness to become fully manifest in your life because of how time works (more on this later), but you would know—instantly—that you are free. That is exactly what I experienced in that single moment where I understood everything in a flash. That moment, in essence, was the end of all my healing, at the spiritual level. It was my moment of re-enlightenment, so to speak.

But I want to tell you more about love, not myself.

WHAT IS LOVE?

Love is not a feeling. It is not just an emotion you experience from time to time. It certainly has nothing to do with any kind of relationship you may have with someone or something other than yourself. Love isn't something that requires two or more people to come together. All of these misunderstandings and re-definitions of the word love have come about because most people don't have what it takes to experience love first hand and understand for themselves what it really is. Unfortunately, humanity has always redefined things that are difficult to attain in much shallower ways so that it doesn't feel left behind or abandoned by the universe, and the experience of love is one of those things. You can experience love all the time, but only if you live at a very high level of intelligence and energy, which is essentially what all enlightened beings do.

BUT IF LOVE IS NOT A FEELING, WHAT IS IT?

Love is a force, and the highest form of intelligence that exists in this existence, in any other existence, or beyond. In my spiritual experience, it was clear to me that love was *dissolving* clouds of consciousness into nothing, absolute zero. Love was pervading every cloud and slowly turning everything that it touched into nothing. This is the process of love, in action. Love is the reason our universe, as well as every other universe, is expanding. It is the reason why everything on this Earth is getting subtler and thinner, spiritually speaking. It is the reason why humanity has been getting more and more intelligent as time passes, even though it has not figured out how to use its intelligence properly. Love is the reason I am here and the reason I am going to help you become part of the process of dissolution, whereby all of you learn to *let go* and allow what you don't need to be dissolved by love.

In other words, I am here to love you.

It doesn't matter what you believe about the world and the people in your life. If you are a young person that is interested in moving forward spiritually, I want you to know this much: you can count on my love for you, anytime, anywhere. Even if no one else loves you, I do.

Don't think that I am being sentimental, or that I am trying to comfort you. Love is a force of *dissolution*, which means that if you come to me in person and receive my love, you will become *less* than who you were before you met me. If you let me love you, things will disappear from your life. Everything that is excessive in your life will start to fall apart, sometimes in ways you don't like (e.g., someone steals your TV—I mean it). This is what love does, and has always done. It has replaced everything you don't need with the only thing you really need: love itself.

Why? As I said, love is the highest form of intelligence. If you have love in your heart, it means you are functioning at the peak of your intelligence. It means that no matter where you are and how little you have, you will find a way to do what you care about, every moment of your life, guaranteed. You will navigate your life with more ease than a lizard navigates this Arizona landscape I find myself in as I write this. You will not come across obstacles in your life at all because your intelligence will navigate you *subconsciously* in a way that eliminates all need for you to deal with obstacles. Every single thing in your life—including yourself—will *literally* be in the right place, at the right time, all the time. It doesn't matter how much the world changes around you—nothing will be a challenge for you.

PERFECTION IS POSSIBLE

If you've read this far, it means you've chosen to walk the path of light, and the consequence of walking the path of light is intelligent living. You can be sure that all the people that choose the path of darkness will never, ever come close to living as beautifully as you will, even if you have far fewer resources than they do.

I was asked to write this book because you need to know that this is possible even today, because this is how I live my life. As I write this, I am sitting in total peace on a beautiful sunny day in Tucson. It is very warm— just how I like it. There are birds tweeting, flowers blooming, the pleasing sound of a garbage truck in the distance (yes, I find the noise of the world pleasing!). The keyboard on my little laptop makes cute clacking noises as my fingers effortlessly move across the keys. I don't have to think about what I am writing because the words just flow like a gentle waterfall. The occasional breeze makes the plants bob and dance, while a butterfly flutters around. And there is a funny little roadrunner hunting for lizards around me.

Everything—I mean everything—is absolutely perfect.

This is the kind of life I want all of you to live, and it is possible for every single one of you, no exceptions. The details of your life will vary, of course. Perhaps you like cooler weather and prefer to live in the mountains. Perhaps you like to travel while it's raining. Perhaps you wish to plant an orchard and work with animals. Whatever it may be, it will happen, because when the highest level of intelligence is functioning on your behalf, it makes every single thing absolutely perfect, and works *relentlessly* to keep it that way.

All *you* have to do in order to get there is give in.

SURRENDER IS THE GOAL

This book is ultimately about helping you surrender, but I am not here to tell you to surrender to Jesus or to God. I am going to give you practical advice on how you can raise your intelligence gradually, until you come across a barrier you can cross only if you allow love to take over from that point onwards. In other words, I am going to teach you how to live so that you can *invite* love—the highest form of intelligence—to come into your life and guide your every move.

Oh yes, you will have a choice as to whether or not to invite love into your life. Everyone that has walked the spiritual path has been given that choice. But I won't lie to you: no one refuses love once they get to that point. No one. To give you an analogy, walking the path of light is like walking in 110-degree heat for hours to get to a bus stop: once you get there, you will not refuse to get on the bus and continue in comfort.

Which brings me to the truth about walking the path of light: it is not easy, as I've warned you once already but will do so many times. Once you get on the bus, everything is easy, but getting to the bus stop is quite difficult. Is that because life is meant to be a challenge, or a test? No, life is not meant to be a challenge, or a test. It's just that most people refuse to let go of things that are trying to leave them so they can move forward with fewer burdens. They keep holding onto their relationships, their possessions, their career, their hobbies, their memories—you name it. Holding onto things drains energy. Meanwhile, love comes in spurts, and whenever it does, even in a small way, it will take away something from your life—guaranteed. Sometimes these will be things you will get back later, but in that moment, you will have to let them go without knowing if you will ever see them again. For many people (especially girls), these moments are wrenching, to say the least.

LOVE IS ABSOLUTE

The thing about love is this: it will enter your life only if you are willing to have love in your life, and nothing else. The keyword here is *willing*. I, for example, have given up every single thing in my life many times *literally*, by putting all my possessions out on the street, only to have someone else take them away within minutes. I have done this 7 times in my life, each time totally changing my looks, lifestyle, hobbies, place of residence, possessions, friends, work environment—everything. I was made to do this so I could live in many, many different ways and be exposed to a huge range of experiences so that I may share all that I am sharing with you, as proof that love is real, that it works, that it's good and that you, too, can have it.

Plus, I have gotten most of what I gave up back again! I didn't plan on these things coming back to me, and I certainly did not foresee them doing so. I am not talking about just the little things like headphones and a piano (yes, love takes care of the little things too), but skills, energy, answers to questions I used to have—everything. Honestly, things are still coming back to me slowly, so my life has never stopped being an adventure: just the way I like it.

Typically, I talk to human beings about love last, after giving them a boatload of guidance on what to do, how to live, etc. But in this case, I need you to accept the fact that walking the path of light is basically walking the path of love. Despite all the warnings I've given you, it is still the easiest path of all, but also the most emotionally devastating. It especially leaves many women in tatters as they fail to come to grips with the truth: everything must go, everything will end. Only love will remain and that too will dissolve in your experience when you dissolve.

COME TO ME

So, if you are a woman, I will give you this option to make things a bit easier: come live with me, assuming you meet the following conditions.

If you are a young woman willing to dedicate your whole life to serving womankind, by walking the path of love and sharing all that you discover along the way—as well as after you are enlightened—with the women of the world, and if, after enlightenment, you promise to continue to serve humanity in whatever capacity you choose, you may live with me for the rest of your life. I will take care of all your needs: food, shelter, clothing, love and wisdom.

The world sorely needs *enlightened mothers* to guide the children to come. No one else can guide the children that are going to arrive in the future. You must be willing to be one of those enlightened mothers.

Do not think I am offering some kind of refuge or escape from the world. Living with a yogi 24/7 is no joke. The usual pleasures, comforts, sex, etc. will not be available to you, nor will you have the traditional experiences of womanhood, such as becoming a mother. I don't have a TV, radio or internet in my home. Until you finish your journey, your contact with the outside world will be limited to working with women only. Even though you will have ample time for rest, sleep and rejuvenation, you will work harder than anyone else on the planet. You will live in silence for most of your life, because I work energetically and need neither words nor touch to help you. Your relationship with me will be little more than your relationship with the Sun—I will simply be a source of light for you—but living constantly in the Sun is not for the faint-hearted or the weak. The more you progress, the deeper your surrender to love will become and at some point, all of your personal dreams, hopes, aspirations and ambitions will simply disappear, never to return. Plus, none of the qualities the world normally thinks are of value (e.g., looks, skills, education) will be of any use on the journey.

Understand that I've been asked to turn my home into an Ashram so that women may take over as soon as possible. I am here to be a source of love and wisdom, not a leader. *As a woman, serving humanity means leading humanity.* This is true even if you don't come to me. I am here to share a message, help the few that can be helped and go home.

The benefit to living with me is that your journey will be on hyper-drive, so to speak. You will finish in 5 years, or less. But you will have to share narratives of your journey with the world *as you are progressing* so that the world may see what it's like for a woman to walk the path of love.

I am not allowed to offer this option to the boys, because first of all, the boys don't need it and second, going through the spiritual journey at such a furious pace that you would finish in 5 years means that *I* have to keep your energy system stable as you hurtle through time. In this area, all the training and guidance I have received is from the Divine Feminine and She has given me intimate knowledge on how to take care of the energy system only in women. Sorry!

Does this mean that those who don't live with me will take a lot longer? Yes. If you decide to walk the path on your own, do not worry if you don't finish in this lifetime. Finishing quickly requires *total* commitment to the work, something few are interested in doing—most people want to enjoy the world at least a little bit along the way. However, your commitment to the path will have an enormous impact on your children, as well as on all the people that come in touch with you in some way. They, in turn, will impact the people in their lives, and so on. Spiritual endeavor hasn't ever been a short-term deal. All of us yogis are constantly planting seeds that are likely to bear fruit in several hundred years, at least. I hope that you are committed to walking the path of light no matter how long it takes, at least for your children's sake.

So now that you have some idea of what you've decided to get into, I will delve into the only quality you need in order to succeed.

COMMITMENT

The first thing that people think about when they hear the word commitment is that it's something you *give*, either to someone else, or to something else. The world has convinced people that commitment is a sort of contract, something that you decide to sign at the cost of your own happiness, well-being, prosperity, livelihood or something else. This is not the kind of commitment you need to succeed on the path of light.

The only thing you, as a human being, should be committed to is your own well-being, health and happiness. Regardless of where you live, what you do or how you want to live your life, if you aren't committed to your own well-being, you will live very poorly, even if you have tons of material wealth.

Do not confuse "well-being" to mean the kinds of things that the world is talking about. The world's idea of well-being has to do entirely with products, services, experiences and things that you buy in order to stay well. *None* of the things that the world is talking about will have a meaningful impact on your well-being. No, not even raw, organic food, meditation or a yoga class. Don't waste your money and time.

THE FUNDAMENTAL MISUNDERSTANDING

There has been a fundamental misunderstanding about the nature of the human being that has caused all sorts of things, experiences and practices to be either concocted or repurposed as solutions to a problem that doesn't exist. This fundamental misunderstanding has been bandied about as truth and it comes in many different forms, but it is essentially this: that there is something wrong with the human being to begin with. In the past, this was expressed using terms such as 'sin' but nowadays it is being expressed in a more subtle and devious fashion. More people now than ever believe that "there is always room for improvement," or that they should be "striving to become a better person." The vast majority of humanity is operating under the assumption that human beings are *essentially flawed*.

But the truth that yogis have always communicated is very simple: there is nothing wrong with the human being and there *has never been* anything wrong with the human being. It is only the idea of sin, the idea of flaw, the idea of imperfection that needs elimination, not sin, flaw or imperfection itself, because the latter doesn't exist.

Once the *idea* of imperfection takes root though, it becomes internalized to a point where human beings operate as if imperfection is a shared experience: at this point everyone seemingly *knows* that everyone is flawed. It is a shared delusion, a universal belief in the helplessness, stupidity and sinfulness of humanity. Over time, this problem has taken on many different forms and has many different names: lack of peace and serenity, lack of happiness, lack of meaning, lack of purpose, lack of connection, depression, anxiety, addiction, suicidal behavior, etc. And now, the whole world is trying to solve these problems in a million different ways.

None of the aforementioned things are problems, but rather, simply an abnormal condition of the human being. These are imbalances in the human system, caused due to one part of the human mechanism being burdened unnecessarily. And the burden is simply *a wrong idea*, which has now exploded into an entire ecosystem of bad ideas that are weighing humanity down. When these burdens become so heavy that a human being finds it unable to live well, it then becomes dependent on support systems in order to even see a way forward in day-to-day situations. Taken together, these support systems are what we are calling *our civilization*.

Don't misunderstand me. I am not saying that civilization *in general* is bad. For example, *shelter* is a fantastic thing. Without it, we would definitely be far less happy. However, *most* of what we've created in civilization is unnecessary, excessive, useless and harmful, because it perpetuates the myth that the human being is flawed and cannot survive without support.

THE TRUTH ABOUT YOU

The fundamental truth about the human being is that in its normal state, a human being is healthy, happy, peaceful, non-violent, serene, purpose-driven, has meaning, finds connection everywhere and has absolutely no issues with life on this Earth. I know this because this has been my state all my life *on the inside* and now, increasingly, on the outside as well. While I was put through a lot of miserable life experiences among really sick people, I wasn't ever unhappy, unhealthy, depressed or anxious on the inside. I never had issues with finding connection and never questioned the meaning or purpose of life. The beauty of life always has revealed itself to me as easily as the morning sun reveals the world in which we live. In other words, life is perfect and to me, that is a fact as clear as daylight. I didn't need to meditate, take drugs, exercise or sit in front of a guru in order to get there, because I have always been there.

All you have to do to experience the freedom, the love and the clarity with which you are expected to operate *naturally*, is to unburden yourself from all that is weighing you down. This is the exact opposite of what the world wants you to do. The world wants you to buy supports and counterweights so you can keep carrying the burden you have, and take on some more—everything from houses and cars, to drugs and cosmetics, toys and entertainment, you name it. But what you really need to do is to steadily *give up* these supports and learn to walk on your own two feet.

That, in essence, is the process of enlightenment. That is what the spiritual journey is all about. It isn't about coming in touch with God, talking to Jesus or gaining superpowers. It isn't about exploring the secrets of the cosmos, becoming a Goddess or coming up with some new yogic technology. It isn't about healing the planet, saving animals or becoming a better person.

Fundamentally, spirituality means that you give up all kinds of false identities, beliefs, ideas, prejudices, opinions—everything holding you back—and identify with the *spirit*, that is to say, with who you really are, free from all the narratives that have been layered upon you to make you believe that you are a this, or a that. And that is quite a difficult journey for most people simply because they *like* these other identities.

Most people find it comforting to pretend to be someone other than who they really are, because it allows them to feel like they're hiding behind a mask and thereby feel safe. Therefore, even though the feeling of safety is false, people find the prospect of having to give up their pretense more frightening than death itself!

If you want to be free, invite love into your life and live in a beautiful way, you *must* commit to one thing, and only one thing: raising your intelligence. Only when your intelligence rises can you give up what is false, because intelligence infuses your whole body with courage. Only when your intelligence rises can you distinguish truth from fiction, even as the kinds of fiction evolve and become ever more complex and intricate. Only when your intelligence rises can you stay balanced as the world continues to become more disorganized and out of control. And this whole process of raising your intelligence starts with one thing: you must stop believing that there is something wrong with you. In Chapter 5, I will describe how to put this into practice.

SELF-CENTEREDNESS IS ESSENTIAL

In general, people believe that being selfish is a bad thing, that focusing on one's own life, one's own success or one's own goals to the exclusion of others is evil. In fact, the exact opposite is true. People who focus on others fall into two camps: they are either people like me who have been asked to serve and enlighten humanity, or they are people who've got nothing worthwhile in their own lives and constantly need to focus on others. People who live beautiful lives never focus on others. Let me give you an example.

The first time that visitors encounter the Grand Canyon in person, they are completely awestruck, baffled by its sheer size and bewildered by its complexity. In addition to all the details, such as the colors of the rocks, the many varied landscapes and the serenity, people are silenced by the sheer beauty of the place. This is what happens to almost everyone who stands on the edge of the rim for the first time.

Do you think, at that moment, that any of these people are thinking about someone else?

We are wired to be utterly mesmerized by truth, beauty and love. Whenever we experience these things, even if only for a fleeting moment, we become *totally* engrossed in it. Many of us crave these moments, not realizing that the experience of truth, beauty and love is created from within us and that it is ever-present. In order to experience beauty, all you need to do is shift your focus away from all that is ugly and towards all that is beautiful. This shift is made more easily in places like the Grand Canyon, but you don't need to live at the Grand Canyon in order to experience it. What you need to do is train your body to focus on what is true, beautiful and lovable anywhere and everywhere. This is yet another thing that happens when you raise your intelligence.

Living a beautiful life isn't about accumulating pretty things, pretty people and nice experiences. It isn't about earning enough money so that you can spend all your time at the Grand Canyon or out on the Pacific Ocean being mesmerized by the Earth's beauty. Living a beautiful life means that your experience of life is beautiful no matter what is going on. As I will explain later in this book, this takes enormous amounts of *power*, power that your body will find within itself if given enough time and energy to do so.

This is why you *must*, at least as long as you are working on raising your intelligence, be utterly self-centered and not spend even an ounce of your time and energy on other people and their problems. You must be totally committed to your own life, and not at all to anyone else's. I don't care that you have a dog in your life, or that you have children, a husband or wife, or elderly parents that need taking care of. I don't care that you work at a treatment center for addicts, or spend all your energies helping the homeless. I don't care that you are totally interested in saving the ecosystem of this planet.

Neither does the universe.

When you don't understand the big picture, when you don't have the highest level of intelligence operating through you, when your experience of life isn't beautiful, when your focus is on all that is false, ugly and unlovable, everything you do will be simply *wrong*. And this is why the world continues to get worse even though people are working very hard in order to find solutions to problems such as hunger, poverty, homelessness, genocide and so on. In other words, they just don't get it.

It is like the story of the elephant and the blind. Unenlightened people, with limited intelligence and cloudy vision constantly come up with problems that don't exist and then put enormous amounts of time, energy and resources into "solving" them. But the more people apply their limited intelligence to solve problems that *essentially* don't exist, the more imbalances they create worldwide, causing new problems to appear, such as gun violence, drug addiction and teen suicide. The vast majority of human beings, especially the older ones, are too set in their ways to even see the truth of these statements, but you, the young person, *must first* learn to see clearly before you take a step forward. Only if you do that will you do the right thing for everyone.

And that means you must make your first priority—indeed your *only* priority—your spiritual growth, which is the same as achieving well-being, the same as raising your intelligence and the same as inviting love into your life. This takes total self-centeredness.

But do not think that self-centeredness means that you must abandon whatever job or responsibility you have today, such as helping the homeless at a shelter. What you must do is change *how* you go about doing whatever you do.

THE WAY

All spiritual success depends not on what you do, but the way you do it. This simple idea is so misunderstood that most spiritual aspirants apply it in completely the wrong manner. I have met many self-proclaimed "seekers" all across the US and all I've heard from them is some variation of prejudice against one set of people or another. For example, many spiritual aspirants like to claim that they live by a principle of non-violence, which often translates into lifestyle choices such as not eating meat, or being a pacifist, followed quickly by a denunciation of all that eat meat or serve in the military, for example. This is what happens when a human being reads too much spiritual literature without ever having a transformative experience of any sort that shows them the truth of how life is made.

The way our creation is made, there is no right or wrong, good or bad, holy or unholy and so on. Everything that follows the laws of existence is allowed. It's just that some actions will result in suffering and other actions don't, but the difference between actions that cause suffering and actions that don't has nothing to do with the action itself and everything with *the way* that action is performed. Let me give you a simple example.

Imagine for a second that a pretty girl is sitting by herself on a park bench on a beautiful morning. A dog walks by, sniffs the girl's leg, wags its tail and walks off. Then a woman pushing a stroller walks by. The girl notices the baby in the stroller staring at her wide-eyed and smiles. Then comes a little boy, maybe 5 years old, licking an ice cream, and completely oblivious to his surroundings, who waves at the girl as if she is his sister. Finally, another girl walks by, but this time she looks at the girl sitting on the bench up and down, as if to judge her dress sense.

In situations like this, it is clear to everyone that the dog, the baby and the little boy have done nothing wrong, while the second girl has created unnecessary suffering. This is basically what's going on all around the world. We are all allowed to do what we want to do, actually. For example, there is absolutely nothing wrong with admiring a pretty girl sitting on a park bench. There is no spiritual or existential law that says that we should not drink alcohol or that we should have exactly one sexual partner, for example. But the *way* people are going about doing those things, as well as everything else, is causing an enormous amount of suffering in the world, and all of it is totally unnecessary.

I will explain what it means to do things the right way in great detail in this book, because it has nothing to do with the right attitude. It is far deeper than that and takes an elevated level of intelligence to get right. But for now, I want you to understand this much: no matter what you are doing today, you must focus entirely on changing *the way* you do things and not the what. And this book will help you with that every step of the way.

It doesn't matter, for example, that you work at a meat processing plant and slaughter pigs all day. It doesn't matter that you are a female drone pilot in the military that regularly kills people. It doesn't matter that you work in the pornography industry. The path of light is open to you. Yes, it *is* a lot easier to follow the path of light if you don't do those things and instead, spend your days conserving with plants at a national park, for example, because the physical environment in a national park is much nicer. But do not think working at a national park makes you better in some way or even more likely to succeed. Some of the most arrogant people in the world are spiritual aspirants who have decided that they are better than everyone else and therefore stuck. Spiritual development isn't a contest, or a race. So, instead of trying to change your situation, accept your life as it is today and focus on the way you do things.

I will guarantee this much though: as you become more established in doing things the right way, you will find that you will do different things. In other words, *the way* will influence *the what*. When that happens, you must accept whatever changes life brings and move forward.

THE ROLE OF YOGIS, GURUS AND SAINTS

I have been very happy to note that membership and attendance at religious institutions in the US has been falling of late. This is a good sign that people are finally beginning to give up on what hasn't ever worked—relying on a middleman that acts as the arbiter of truth, beauty and love for your sake. You don't need anyone to access the best of what life has to offer, because you were made to receive them effortlessly. Sure, people like me can *accelerate* your journey, but if you aren't in a rush, you don't need me either. All of the spiritual support mechanisms that have been offered by yogis, gurus, saints and the like over millennia are for people who really want to get to the end before they die and still have some time left to actually enjoy a beautiful life on this Earth. If you don't mind spending all your life practicing walking the path of light and *knowing*, when you die, that you did all you could, you would still die fulfilled and happy. For many people, that really is enough—they're ok with just dying in a good state.

But if you want to *live* as much as possible, then you need people like me and a book like this, which is why people like me are always making ourselves available to you for free as much as possible. We don't need you to come and pay your respects, or donate money. However, what we *do* need, for you to succeed, is *absolute commitment* to the goal of raising your own intelligence. This is why, in my life, I simply ignore people that don't commit to themselves. I couldn't care less that someone is in dire straits; if they aren't willing to do anything for themselves, I will only push them further down the path of darkness they've chosen.

No, I am not a sadist—this is actually how the ultimate power in the universe works, which is why I asked you to commit either to the path of darkness, or to the path of light, before proceeding any further. Whichever path you choose, the power that operates in all creation will do its utmost to push you down your chosen path as quickly as possible. That's the law.

This is why people who proceed down the dark path never recover unless someone like a guru or myself intervenes on your behalf. However, it is extremely rare that someone who has enjoyed the pleasures of the world really wants to turn things around. Usually, people just want a bit of comfort and solace when things are really bad. And in situations like that, neither a guru nor a yogi like me will help you, because we don't exist to provide comfort and solace. If you come to us in a state like that, we will make sure that you go down your chosen path even more fervently.

So, don't ever go looking for a guru. If you end up in front of a guru, and you have the wrong intentions, your life may end up becoming a living nightmare, as the guru literally empowers you to go down the path you choose as furiously as possible. If you really need a guru, they will appear in your life. I don't mean that you will get a hint, a suggestion, or a vague sign that you must interpret. I mean that the guru will *literally* appear in your life and direct you towards them in some fashion. Gurus don't often appear in people's lives in human form though, which is why people are confused. Let me tell you a story to help you understand how gurus work.

During the middle part of my 7-year healing period, on a beautiful fall morning in Chapel Hill, North Carolina, I was riding my motorcycle down a busy highway when I felt a huge surge of energy in my body. I nearly lost all consciousness and everything started to fade into white. I thought that

I was about to leave the body and crash my motorcycle, but somehow, I pulled over by the side of the highway on a bridge and got off my motorcycle. I took off my helmet, and leaning on the wall of the bridge, simply stood there with my hands shaking.

This moment was the culmination of several weeks of pondering over a range of experiences that I was having. All of those experiences were supernatural and I was really struggling to make any sense of what was going on. I could neither explain nor share these experiences with others without sounding like a lunatic. Just before the moment that I started to experience a surge of energy on my motorcycle, I had found my answer: Love was coming into my life in amounts I had not experienced before and it was blowing away many of the burdens I had accumulated during the first 33 years of my life while helping others spiritually. If this happened to you, you too would have many supernatural experiences because your brain would fail to make sense of the sudden release.

Literally an hour after I pulled over, my focus started to shift. I began paying attention to some very specific things to the exclusion of other things. One thing led to another, and I found myself opening my laptop and looking straight at a photograph of a guru that was in the US at the time. I knew *instantly* that I had to go see him and until I reserved a spot at the event he was going to be at, my body basically refused to do anything else.

That's how powerful a calling of a guru should be. It should take over and let you know without a shadow of a doubt, that you have to go see them. Otherwise, it's not real.

I am not a guru. I am a Yogi, which means I won't appear in your life and direct you towards me. If you feel strongly enough that you want to meet me, you're welcome to contact me, but I reserve the right to ignore you, because I have a job to do, and that includes meeting only with people who really want to do something good for the benefit of all. I am no longer available in person to those who simply want to progress in their own life.

But the question remains: is it ok for you to go to another yogi, guru or a saint and seek their blessings or their guidance? Sure, but understand that spirituality is not like the US highway system: you don't change lanes to go faster or slower. You must stick to one lane. If you've decided, for example, to follow my guidance, don't look elsewhere or you'll simply get confused. If you've decided to follow the practices of a certain religion, don't read my book or you'll make a mess of your life. Pick something, and stick with it all life long, no matter where it takes you.

NOTHING IS RELATIVE

In real life, nothing is relative. Relativism is something that happens only in narratives. In real life, everything is absolute and your commitment should be also. Now that you've decided to walk the path of light, you must not waver. If you've decided to continue to follow my guidance, don't ever read another religious, spiritual or self-help book, ever again.

Do not think that reading many different opinions will give you a broader perspective. The broadest perspective is one that is all-encompassing, that includes, appreciates and integrates all there is in life and beyond into a holistic understanding. This type of understanding is not relative—it is absolute. You will not understand a little bit about everything, but everything about something and nothing more. Most of life will remain a mystery to you, and that's a good thing. At the same time, you will know whatever it is you need to know, when you need to know it and never be confused. This is called knowing by being. It is a state you have to experience to understand.

Once your intelligence starts to rise, you will understand that even though there are many ways to look at the same thing, there are no two ways that are in conflict with each other and still correct. All enlightened perspectives are correct, because they are all inclusive, while still focusing only on one particular aspect of life. It's like the story of the elephant and the blind, except this time, everyone can see. One person might describe the elephant in one manner, another in a different manner, but their accounts will not conflict. In real life, nothing is opposed to anything else. Everything works together.

Living in reality, meaning living in the absolute, will make your life easy, because you will no longer care about what isn't yours to care about. You will neither compare, contrast, nor judge because you will not even see what isn't yours to see. Your life becomes utterly focused on what you love and you will find it impossible to be distracted by the world. Once that happens, you are essentially *committed by nature*, not by effort.

Now that I've laid enough of a foundation for you to start wondering what we're going to do here, let's get started with some basics you need to understand.

HOW LIFE WORKS

YOUR BODY

The popular scientific narrative about the body goes something like this: your body is a biological entity separate from the rest of the universe and has independent, free will. The brain controls many aspects of the body and in addition to managing physical systems, allows for faculties like language and decision making. The body we can see is all there is and at the end of life, when the body ends, it's all over. Therefore, it's imperative that we keep the body running as best as we can, as long as we can.

If my experience of life had been nothing more than whatever fits that description, I would agree, but it hasn't been. Nor has it been the life experience of millions of yogis, mystics, saints, gurus and even ordinary people from all walks of life. We all know there is more to it, much more. Some of us deny that and choose to find a biological or scientific explanation for all experiences. However, there isn't anything I can say to convince you one way or another as to what the reality of life really is. You must experience it for yourself and decide if the popular scientific narrative is of value.

All yogis speak about life entirely based upon their own experience. None of us are interested in talking about it from another yogi's point of view. Accordingly, I will share with you how it is that life is made based on many spiritual and physical experiences I've had. If you do read another yogi's account, you will find that we aren't in conflict in any way.

LAYERS OF THE BODY

Essentially, life is a continuum. There is no such thing as "the body," strictly speaking, but in order to make it easier for us to understand what is going on, we typically speak about the body, as well as all of life, as being more discrete than it really is. In that sense, there are many different layers that are of interest to yogis of various kinds, but I am only here to share with you a simplified version that is more than sufficient for you to progress on the spiritual path, and create a beautiful life and a happy world.

There are only 3 layers that you need to pay attention to: Physicality, Energy and Emotions.

The physical body is what you are all used to seeing, touching, etc. It is what you see when you look in the mirror, and generally what you see growing when you get stronger and shrinking when you get weaker. The energy body is something you cannot see, but many of you feel it. Most people can tell the difference between feeling exhausted *on the inside*, and feeling tired, *on the outside*. When you are exhausted, life seems dull and drab. When you are energetic, things are interesting and worth exploring. This is different from feeling tired, which can happen even if you are in a good mood. And finally, there is the emotional body, which is really only interesting to those with an elevated level of femininity, such as most women and others such as myself who have integrated the feminine within themselves. I will speak about this more in later chapters.

Many yogis and gurus in the past have used the word "mind" to describe one of the layers of the body. I will not use that word in my descriptions or even practices, because there is no such thing as "the mind." It is simply a collection of faculties your body has that yogis in the past focused on as a way of helping people make progress spiritually. However, life has changed and we no longer need to speak about "the mind." Accordingly, I will always only speak about the body and its layers.

THE BODY IS LIKE A BUILDING

The energy layer in your body is like the foundation of a building. It is the layer on which your physical body is built. Just like most buildings in the real world, you cannot see the foundation, but if something is wrong with it, you will definitely know at some point, because the visible part of the building will react and respond to whatever's going on in the foundation. The size of the building, its strength, resilience—indeed all the characteristics of a building that we count on—are dependent on having a good strong foundation.

Your experience of life is entirely dependent on whether both the foundation as well as the building on top of it are built well, are well-balanced and resilient in the face of the forces of nature acting upon them. This is important because just like a building, your body has absolutely no control over the surrounding environment. However, just as a building has an influence on what goes on around it, your body has a great deal of influence on its surroundings.

Similar to the many systems that are needed in order to keep a building upright and in good condition, your body comes with everything necessary to be in tip top condition all lifelong. Plus it can do something that an ordinary building cannot do, which is to fix itself, change itself, rebuild itself and so on.

Of course, such self-healing buildings will be constructed in our civilization at some point as well. How can I be so confident? Because of how our world is created.

HOW THE WORLD IS CREATED

When I say "the world," I am only talking about the human-made part of the world, not the Sun and the Moon, the weather, trees, animals and the like. The world, as you see it, is entirely a human creation. In fact, it is not wrong to say that you see a world that is unique to you because of the many different ideas, beliefs, opinions and prejudices you carry that shape how you view the world. But before we go there, let's talk about the world you see *on the outside,* so to speak—things like cars, buildings and the many systems that are in place in order to support our civilization.

Every single thing that humanity has created has come out of its understanding of the body and how it functions. When human beings understand the body in a certain manner, they create objects, systems, philosophies, religions and even spiritual practices in keeping with that kind of understanding. This is because we can only see and experience life through the body and all our creations are made to respond to the world around them in a manner consistent with our understanding of how the body responds to its surroundings. This *understanding* does not have to be conscious. In fact, most of what humanity has understood so far, has remained subconscious and this subconscious understanding of life is what is driving human endeavor throughout the world. Depending on what someone understands and how well they understand it, they create something out of that understanding and it becomes a part of the world in which we live.

For example, as long as humanity assumed that the human body was a machine that breathed air, burned fuel and moved, we created a certain kind of machine called the internal combustion engine that is still in use everywhere. Once we began encountering a whole different kind of understanding as to how the body's power source works, we came up with electric cars. As long as our understanding of the body's communication mechanism remained mechanical, we used primitive ways of communication in the world, such as pigeons or even cables carrying electrical signals. Once our understanding evolved, we came up with things such as radio and microwave transmission.

It is a great fallacy to think that technological progress is a result of science. Science is simply one way of *narrating* our understanding of how life works. It is understanding that comes first and science, like every other field of expression such as art and philosophy, merely follows. But what causes our understanding to change?

Simply the fact that everything is becoming more intelligent over time.

ENERGY, INFORMATION AND INTELLIGENCE

All that exists in creation can be described using three attributes: energy, information and intelligence. This is a yogic point of view, so do not think of this as an alternative to scientific literature. There is nothing wrong with the scientific narrative that describes the universe as made up of particles and waves, for example—it is simply a limited point of view that relies on measurement of only the physical aspects of the universe. The yogic point of view, however, spans not just the physical but also the non-physical aspects of life, the latter being something science has yet to acknowledge in any meaningful way.

According to this yogic point of view, energy gives something mass, or substance. For example, you, as a human being, have more energy than a house cat. Information gives something structure, or rigidity. For example, a rock has more information in it than air. And finally, intelligence influences behavior, i.e., the ability of something to respond to life. The more intelligent something is, the more sophisticated its response is to the environment around it.

Taken together, these three things—energy, information and intelligence—can be used to describe the nature of just about everything in existence and beyond. The three attributes are subtle, of course, in the sense that you cannot perceive them easily. For instance, you can see the *effect* of energy on something, but you cannot see energy itself. But when energy is mixed with information to give it structure, suddenly an object is perceived. And when intelligence is added to that object, it starts to behave in a particular manner instead of remaining totally inert.

It is not important for you to understand all the ways in which these three attributes interact, but you must know this: the level of energy and intelligence in our universe is increasing and the level of information is decreasing.

Recall the experience of love I described in the beginning of Chapter 2. Our universe is expanding. As intelligence grows, everything becomes subtler, and as things become subtler, they become less rigid. All existence is slowly becoming *less and less*, in the sense that it is essentially turning into nothing. But at the same time, everything in existence is becoming more intelligent over time, even rocks and trees. Across our universe, the level of information is decreasing and the level of intelligence is increasing.

This is what we are calling the process of evolution, except evolution isn't just a physical process and happens at all levels. In fact, the primary evolutionary process that has been in play on this Earth has not been physical, but spiritual. While human beings have remained more or less the same in a physical sense for a while now, the level of intelligence among human beings (and other creatures), has been growing at a very fast rate.

But if that's the case, why haven't the animals and plants also created a civilization of their own, or added to ours? Because we are receptive to intelligence in a way that they are not.

RECEPTIVITY IS KEY

The body of a rock, a plant or an animal is limited in a way that prevents it from being receptive to intelligence, not just at a physical level but at other levels as well. This is essentially the magic that evolution has performed on this Earth—it has evolved the creatures of this planet until *we* came along. Our bodies are the pinnacle of what is possible in this universe by evolving things at a physical level. By the way, when I say "physical" here, I am including the energy system of the human being, which is also at its peak and cannot evolve further.

It is because of our superior evolution that we are *far* more receptive to the way life is evolving spiritually than anything else on this Earth, meaning that we are able to grow in intelligence as much as the universe will allow, while the rest of the creatures on this planet will only receive a much smaller boost over time. While we can actually experience the magic of life in a billion different ways, the rest of the creatures on this planet have to make do with whatever their bodies are capable of at the physical level and therefore do little more than eat, sleep and procreate.

It is because we are becoming more intelligent and more subtle that we have come up with technologies like social media, that we have art in our civilization or that we spend most of our lives engaging with concepts and ideas. This is the reason we have all these inventions now, why our civilization is changing faster and faster, why we are coming up with new ways of looking at life and why we are all trying so hard to make the world a better place.

I actually find it strange that there are people in the US who think evolution is somehow anti-spiritual, because it is in fact evolution that makes spirituality possible for human beings. But what is spirituality anyway and what does it have to do with all this?

SPIRITUALITY IN A NUTSHELL

Spirituality isn't a belief system, nor is it a set of practices. Spirituality fundamentally means only one thing: identification with the spirit, not anything else. Let me take you through a simple exercise to help you understand.

Look around you. Most likely you have your phone or some electronic device nearby. When you look at it, it's clear to you that that device isn't you, right? You are not the device.

Now shift your focus to your own hands. When you look at your hands, do you see yourself, or do you see a pair of hands?

Most people, if they've never tried an exercise like this before, will look at their hands and say "this is me." But if you didn't have hands (say you lost them in an accident), would you somehow be not you or "less" you? You would still be you, right? So, you are not your hands. Or perhaps you prefer to say that your hands are a part of you, but they are not you.

This kind of thing is brought home very starkly to patients who are about to die and are hooked up to medical devices keeping them alive. Even if a person is unable to move, speak, open their eyes or even breathe by themselves, loved ones will often look at them and say "they are still there." They don't need convincing. They know. Only when someone is "brain dead" do doctors usually give up all hope, because according to our current medical understanding, a person that is brain dead will never "regain consciousness." Unfortunately, while this understanding is wrong, it will be a while before modern medicine starts to seriously consider separating the condition where the body is not functioning from the condition when one is "physically dead," i.e., when one has left the body permanently. But let's get back to our exercise.

Let's say you fall asleep and start dreaming, do you become someone else? You can, actually. Maybe you watched a movie before falling asleep and in your dream, you became whoever it was you saw in the movie. What does this mean?

It means that your identity is flexible.

For the longest time, people have enjoyed a flexible identity without realizing that what they often do is become so attached to one identity that they forget they can have other identities as well. Performers such as musicians often succumb to this where, after many years of performing on stage, they no longer know themselves as anything but who they are on stage.

Actors often come across as more honest on screen than they do in real life, because many of them identify much more with who they are when they are pretending, than with who they are when they're not. And in American society, most people identify *very* strongly with who they are at work, their political party of choice, their religion, race, gender and so on.

Unfortunately, *none* of these identities are real. These identities are at the mercy of the world around you, because they exist only within the world in which you live. If you lived in the woods, for example, none of those identities would matter. When the world changes, the very foundations of a specific identity can be demolished. This has caused a great deal of consternation lately with gender identity specifically, as some people have struggled to come to terms with identities that don't seem to fall into any of the slots that most of the world has deemed acceptable.

What makes this identity crisis possible is intelligence, unfortunately! An animal that exists at a far lower level of intelligence than a human being does not suffer from an identity crisis. In fact, most animals don't have an awareness of identity as such—they just experience life and that's it. In other words, a lizard cannot see itself as separate from the body, while some other creatures can—chimps, for example. Human beings have been using their intelligence to create new identities, getting lost in them and then living their lives through those identities, instead of as themselves. And because humanity is rising in intelligence, it is getting into more and more trouble with these identities—some on this planet are so consumed by their chosen identity that they barely resemble human beings at this point. Being able to carry an identity when necessary, and then drop it when no longer necessary takes a high level of intelligence, and not all human beings are intelligent enough to do so.

In other words, human beings have evolved into something they don't understand, but instead of first attempting to understanding themselves, they've decided to start experimenting willy-nilly with their intelligence, creating all kinds of havoc.

The thing about an identity crisis of any sort is that it's totally made up. At the end of the day, you must identify with only one thing: yourself. And that means identifying not with a political party, a role in a movie, a persona you take on at work, your body, your "soul" or anything you've heard others speak of. This means that you must strip yourself of all identities that are layered on you by the world without you realizing it, and come back to being yourself. This, in a nutshell, is the end goal of spirituality, nothing more.

However, this is something you will never succeed at doing all by yourself, because you cannot escape a trap that you yourself have laid.

HOW YOUR LIFE IS CREATED

Your life isn't created by a higher power and imposed upon you. There isn't anyone else in charge of your life. Your life isn't set in stone. Destiny doesn't exist. Nothing in this universe is interested in limiting you, and there is no one waiting to judge you for all the things you've done.

All these narratives have come about simply because human beings, in general, don't know how to create a beautiful life—they keep suffering through what seems like a random life that is out of control. They don't know this because they don't know how to use their intelligence. And they don't know how to use their intelligence because they aren't intelligent enough to understand how it works!

Understand this clearly: it is you, the spirit, that has created a certain kind of body and consequently, laid out a series of experiences that you want to enjoy through that body. It is only when you, the spirit, give up identifying with all that isn't you and come back to being yourself, that you will *see a way to change your life.*

In other words, you made a plan for your own life and you are executing it, unknowingly. You have no idea that you are doing this yourself, and because you go about living your life so poorly, you think someone else must be in charge, at least for part of it. It is you that has created all the nonsense you are experiencing—everything from your coffee being at the wrong temperature, to dying unhappy and unfulfilled.

And nobody is going to save you. Why? Because you are, in fact, supposed to have the highest level of intelligence of all the creatures in this universe. Who do you think can possibly save you?

You cannot change your life by changing the world around you, which is basically what everyone is trying to do at this point. This is akin to a building being decorated with bells and whistles or being painted to look different. All that will change when you do this is the appearance of life, not its essence. You will simply end up burdening yourself with more of what the world has to offer, but your experience of life will remain the same.

If you want to change your life, or create a different kind of life, you must tear down the building (including the foundations), and construct a new building, starting from the foundations. This means that you must destroy the energy, intelligence and information that has come together to make your body what it is, and put it all together again in a different way. Or if you prefer, you must *transform* whatever is already built into something completely different.

And there is only one thing that can do that—the power of love.

THE POWER OF LOVE

The power of love isn't something "lovey-dovey," as they say. The power of love is the highest power there is, and in fact, the *only* power that exists. All other kinds of power are essentially derivatives of the power of love. It is this power that people worship as "the ultimate" or sometimes "God." But the power of love neither requires nor cares for your adulation, worship or anything of the sort. It is simply an enabler, something that allows things to happen, that's all.

In fact, it's you.

The shock that many experience when they become spiritually enlightened has to do with the simple truth that they realize that they are, in fact, "God," as most people put it. This shock is great enough to kill, actually, which is why I am only writing all this for the young person who has enough energy to withstand an experience like that. You are, in fact, the ultimate power in the universe, looking through a little window called the human body, experiencing life in a very specific manner and worrying about it.

The masses are "convinced" that this is not true, because most people's idea of power is something they can use to control something else. That's not how the power of love functions. Plus, being one with the ultimate power in the universe would mean that they would have to take responsibility for the way that their life is going. Moreover, they would have to do the hard spiritual work of clarifying their vision, raising their intelligence and living in an intelligent, careful manner for the rest of their lives. If you accept that in fact, you are in charge of the way your life is going, you can no longer pretend to be a victim. You can no longer blame anyone else for what is happening to you because, well, you created the experiences you're enjoying, or enduring—whatever be the case. All of a sudden, every accident, every mishap, every illness, every mistake—all of it is yours!

And the world? All the rapes, murders, genocides, societal ills like addiction, abuse, homelessness, poverty, inequality, war, pollution, climate change—everything would suddenly be your doing. You would have to look out the window and know, with dead certainty, that you did everything you could to make the world the way it is now. Sure, you had lots of collaborators, but you certainly had a hand in making it happen.

Can you handle it?

I hope so, because unless you are willing to accept that whatever is going on in the world is entirely of your own making, you will not make an iota of spiritual progress. Of course, nearly 100% of humanity has decided that denial (and whatever comes along with it, namely an unhappy life and an unfulfilled end) is better. The narratives that you have heard being espoused by the so-called religious, faithful or even spiritual people that say, for example, that you will be saved, that there is a plan for you, that there is a higher power looking out for you, that things will work out, etc. all are bogus. They are lies, misunderstandings and denials of the truth by people who have neither the intelligence, the wisdom, the courage, nor the interest to do the right thing, for themselves, or for the rest of the world.

If you are like most people, you will probably have to take some time at this point to come to terms with this. If you find yourself in a deep pit of some sort, then looking in the mirror and knowing that no one else can pull you out of it is devastating, to say the least. In fact, the truth is that by nature, you will keep going down whatever path you've chosen, which means that in order to progress, you have to climb uphill. If you have really internalized the message that I have shared with you so far, you will experience grief, pain, loss, anger—you name it. It will not be easy, but only those who stop despairing and actually want to do something about life will even take the first step towards freedom.

So, take your time. Don't rush. When you're ready, turn to the next chapter.

FIX YOUR IDENTITY

BEING YOURSELF

In Chapter 3, I asked you to stop believing that there is something wrong with you and later described to you who you really are, from a yogic perspective. While it is nice to know that you are in fact, the ultimate power in the universe (at some level), it isn't enough. Intellectual agreement or acceptance isn't the same as enlightenment, even though many have deluded themselves into thinking it is. The spiritual process doesn't simply convince you that you are what you are, it changes you fundamentally so that you *become* yourself.

In truth, there is no such thing as becoming oneself though, as one is always oneself—what else *can* one be but oneself? When I say "be yourself," I am simply asking you to stop identifying with what you are not. Once your identity is fixed, in the sense that you identify with who you really are, as opposed to whatever is in your experience (e.g., the body, or a job role), then you will stop interfering in the process of life's evolution and allow things to happen easily and naturally. All you have to work on, therefore, is fixing your identity, which is something that needs to be done at multiple layers. It isn't just your psyche that's confused, but your physical body and your energy as well, which is why it is so hard to snap out of it.

Now the philosophical types, which include the yogis who traditionally espoused the path of inquiry (Jnana) have said things like 'All you have to do, is do nothing'. While I understand what they're saying (and they're right), most of you are way too conditioned at this point to even know what it means to do nothing. For me, doing nothing (really doing nothing, not even thinking), came so naturally that when a guru asked me to do nothing, I just sat there blank. But for you this is impossible, so I would advise you not to give in to ridiculous instructions like that which don't work for most people.

This whole book is about practices, but the kinds of practices that work in the real world, as opposed to in some kind of Ashram situation. I will share with you practices that work at every layer, but for now, let's start with the psyche.

THE PRACTICE

In order to fix your identity psychologically, simply change the way you ask questions about yourself.

For instance, let's say you wake up in the morning and don't feel well. Instead of asking yourself "What is wrong with me?," ask yourself "There is nothing wrong with me, so why do I feel unwell?" When you do this, you're saying that you are not your feelings, but there are some bad feelings in your experience and you want to understand why.

Or, let's say that you spilled some coffee on your dress on the way to work. Instead of saying "I am such an idiot!," say to yourself "There is nothing wrong with me, so why did that just happen?" Again, you are separating yourself from your life experience and asking the question of why your life experience is the way it is. You are not even saying that *you* spilled the coffee, but that you experienced a situation where the coffee spilled on your dress.

Or, let's say that you give a nice presentation (or a bad one, doesn't matter) and your boss criticizes you. Instead of blaming yourself, ask yourself, "There is nothing wrong with me, so why am I experiencing this?" Once again, you are separating yourself from whatever the world is up to and asking a question about your life experience.

MAKE IT THE WORLD'S PROBLEM

What you do when you separate yourself from your life experience, is make everything that is going wrong no longer a problem for you to solve. Make all your problems the responsibility of the world you live in, because in fact there isn't anything wrong with you. Once you begin to assume that there is nothing wrong with you, you can actually start to feel that you, in fact, deserve the best: that you should be in perfect shape, have great balance, be focused on what you care about and be happy. Begin to assume that only good things should happen to you. Begin to assume that only good, uplifting, honest and beautiful human beings should be in your life. Begin to assume that everything you need should come to you for free. And most importantly, make all of this the *world's problem*, not your problem.

However, don't go out and start complaining that the world needs to treat you better, or that it needs to change. That's called entitlement and it makes the world a horrible place to live.

All spiritual work happens *inside the body*, in silence. All you need to do is to convince yourself that nothing is wrong with you, but that something is wrong with the world, *and then keep quiet*. I will explain how this works, but it's important that you do the right thing, stop believing that there's something wrong with you, and then keep quiet, no matter what the world says or does.

For most of you, this will be a really difficult challenge in the beginning. The world will constantly want to draw you into an argument, or want to make you work in order to make the world a better place. If you do nothing, the world will blame all of its problems on you, call you names, maybe turn you into a scapegoat. The world in which you live today will do everything it can to make you feel like you are the one responsible for it all. And the world is right—you are, in fact, responsible for the way the world is today. That does not mean the world has any idea how to make it better. And *every* idea the world presents as a solution to the problems it is facing will be wrong, no exceptions. You must not accept the world's suggestions on how to make it a better place. You must not listen to the world at all.

What does this mean in practice? All those ads you see asking for charity, all those calls for volunteers, all those pleas for disaster aid, all those job postings claiming to be focused on creating a better world, all those claims by people and corporations that they are in it for the good of all—all of them are bogus, nonsensical and wrong. In fact, most people engaged in such activities believe they're doing good and don't realize they are only making things worse.

This is where self-centeredness plays a big role. Understand that your life is all that matters. You don't have to go out and change the world, not even to make the world a better place. The world—and all the people that slave for the world's sake—are constantly coming up with arguments for why more involvement, more action and more work is the solution to humanity's problems. But the exact opposite is true. Paradoxically enough, the *less* you contribute to the world, the better it will be. This will make sense as you keep reading, but for now let's focus on what it will do for you.

SHIFT THE BODY'S FOCUS

Once you start to separate yourself from the life you live today and start to assume that whatever problems exist aren't yours to solve, you will begin to make a *huge* shift in the way you live. Once you start to externalize your problems, your body's focus will begin to shift. If there is, in fact, nothing you can do to make the world a better place, why would the body focus on it? So, instead of focusing on all that is wrong in the world, its focus will shift inward, to a place where it feels healthy, happy, safe and secure. Your body will decide that there's no point in focusing on the world's chaos and it will look for the most peaceful, serene place it can find. It just so happens that this place is within you, so your body's focus will shift from the outside to the inside.

As the body focuses inward, it will start to encounter the subconscious, which is chaotic and messy. Continue practicing, and the body will start to dig deeper and look for a more peaceful place to focus. It will go past the psyche, past the subconscious, past the energy layers, deeper and deeper still.

This will go on and on, until one fine day, it will focus on you, the real you, who you really are—the spirit. On that day, your identity will become one with yourself, as opposed to whatever else you have been telling yourself you are. As soon as that happens, you will find yourself at peace-totally, permanently and unwaveringly at peace. You will literally be able to read a book or do a crossword puzzle in the middle of a warzone if you wish. This process will take a long time though—decades maybe—so don't expect results on day one.

How does this work? Let me give you an analogy.

Imagine for a second that all of life is an ocean. At the surface, the ocean is usually quite choppy and chaotic, especially if there is a storm. Unlike a body of water that is never disturbed, the ocean is constantly responding to everything happening throughout the planet (and beyond!) and there-fore, always in motion. Sitting on the surface of the ocean isn't exactly the calmest experience in the world. In fact, many people get sick thanks to the constant motion.

But if you dive into the water, you will find that just under the surface, there is a lot going on (there's often more life just underneath the surface) and at the same time, it's more stable. There are fewer waves and it's definitely not as choppy. If you keep diving deeper and deeper, eventually you will come to a place which is almost completely still, quiet, dark and peaceful.

This is basically what your body will do. So far, your body has been totally focused on the chaotic, choppy and stormy nature of the world. Whether you call it "other people," the news, social media, your job, your health or whatever else, your body has been constantly barraged by the nonstop nonsense it encounters at the very surface of life on this Earth. Once you start separating yourself from what's going on, it will start to look deeper until it finds a place where things are absolutely still, calm, serene and unmoving. While an ocean actually cannot manage to be totally still at any level, there is a level within you—what we are calling 'the spirit'--that is absolutely unmoving and still. Once your body is totally focused at that level, it will not ever be disturbed by anything that happens in the world. *That* is the end goal of spirituality, because what has happened then, is that your identity has been fixed.

THE CONSEQUENCE

Once your identity is fixed, your body is no longer disturbed and able to calmly understand everything it needs to understand, figure out what to do and do it. In other words, it becomes *free*. As soon as this happens, *you* experience freedom like never before, because your entire life experience is dependent on the body through which you are experiencing life. Give the body a place to focus, be at peace and give it the freedom it needs and all of a sudden, it will magically fix every problem in your life—effortlessly, *and* with zero input required from you. I mean that in a very literal sense. You will wake up one fine day with many of your problems simply gone— people and situations included. As time passes, your body will find more and more ways to simply eliminate every single problem in your life and you will start to live in ways that no one else can make sense of. You will live in a manner utterly unique to you, without encountering a single problem *and* not having to even lift a finger in order to do so. You will just find that the world, the universe and beyond start to present you with options you never had before, because *they* will do the work, not you. And that's how it should be.

THE END OF DOING

You, the spirit, are only given the power to *enable* things to happen, but not the power to *make* things happen, i.e., the power to *do*. That power is given to a different level of intelligence, a level of intelligence that actually manages all that needs managing, fixes things as needed, keeps things in operation, maintains them, etc. There is a level of intelligence in our creation that has been explicitly tasked with this work. And it's always waiting for you to give up trying to control and manipulate things so that it can do things instead, do them well and do them right. It is also a level of intelligence that nearly all of humanity has consistently misunderstood since the beginning of language and as a consequence looked to for guidance, sustenance and other such nonsense. Do you know what I am talking about?

God.

LET GOD DO THE WORK

A TERRIFYING EXPERIENCE

On a beautiful morning in Apex, North Carolina, I was sitting in the home that my wife at the time had decided we should live in and decked out with all sorts of comforts. It's the only time in my life I remember sitting on a couch on a regular basis—normally I like having no furniture in my own home. It just so happened that this couch always caught the best of the sunshine streaming in through the south-facing windows and during those years, I always needed the light and heat. This was towards the end of my healing period, and my body was still very weak, so I would often spend hours sunning myself before I could do even simple things like cook a meal. On this particular day though, the wife was out of town and I was sitting on the couch feeling very serene, but also somewhat apprehensive. Something had been brewing deep inside me for a couple of days or so, which usually meant that I was on the cusp of yet another deep spiritual experience emerging out of me.

Sure enough, as I sat still, I felt a surge of energy—gentle but powerful—coming on and soon, I found myself "lifted" out of my body into a different dimension of experience. As I've said before, spiritual experiences aren't sensory and you don't lose awareness of your surroundings. You could say it's more like "augmented reality," whereby a different dimension of experience uses, adds to, builds on and enhances your existing experience, while clarifying, enlightening and explaining many things—all without a single word being said.

Once I was lifted out of the body, I found myself in front of what I can only describe as an airline cockpit with dials, switches, knobs, controls—you name it—except it went on forever in every direction. Every single control seemed to be meaningful, interactive and in harmony with all the other controls. In a flash I realized that I was looking at my own being—not just the body, but the whole being—and its control mechanism. This being was hurtling through Time at a speed I cannot put in words because, well, anything hurtling through Time itself is beyond Time, so its speed cannot be measured. All I knew was that my being was like a super-craft of some sort that, despite moving at some outrageous speed, was able to maintain perfect balance, with not a single vibration, sound or issue. Then, as I watched with awe, and a bit of trepidation, a terrifying moment arrived.

I was handed control of this craft.

I tell you I have never been so terrified my whole life, even though I wasn't "afraid," as such. It was just a numbing moment where I simply froze and refused to move a muscle. I saw, while I was looking at this cockpit, that every single control was *incredibly* sensitive, that if I made the slightest change in one setting without making sure the other settings were also simultaneously adjusted, that I would probably cause this whole craft to blow up. The speed with which I was flying was unforgiving, which meant that every change had to be made with utter clarity and certainty. I had to know what everything did and how everything would react before making the tiniest adjustment.

There was *no way* I wanted control of this thing.

As soon as I was sure about that, the experience ended as quickly as it came on, and I found myself once again simply sitting on my couch, breathing a sigh of relief.

WHAT GOD REALLY IS

God is not the ultimate power in the universe. There are many names for the ultimate power in different religions—Christ, Allah, Krishna, etc. But God isn't one of them, or at least, it shouldn't be. God is a very specific level of intelligence that is tasked with keeping this mechanism you call "the human being" running. That is *all* God does and all that God has been tasked with.

Most of the time, most of your mechanism is under God's control, but there are a few things that you are in control of that are causing you to go awry. This is a consequence of evolution. As our system ("the human being") evolved, we realized that there are parts of our system we can actually use to manipulate the physical reality around us and we became very enamored with it. Unfortunately, we didn't spend any time trying to understand just how intricate, delicately balanced, sensitive and powerful this human mechanism is. We started to experiment recklessly, not just with ourselves but also with the environment around us, and we've mostly created a train wreck. All the problems you are seeing in the world, as well as the numerous diseases people are suffering from, are all a consequence of us running this mechanism really poorly and experimenting with it in all sorts of stupid ways without understanding it first.

It is time that God be given back control of *the entirety* of your human mechanism so that God can run it properly. Unless God is able to handle every aspect of this mechanism, it is unable to take care of everything perfectly, which is why you see people having so much trouble sometimes even getting through their day. When people use their limited intelligence in order to say, feed, clothe, exercise and balance themselves poorly, God has to compensate for their stupidity in many ways just to keep the mechanism going. Eventually, of course, the whole balancing act fails and things come crashing down. When this happens, death is usually the result, but it can also be things like very bad accidents and such.

Understand that your entire life experience is totally dependent on what you call "the human being" being in tip-top condition, all the time. This means not just eating, sleeping, working and exercising well, but also taking care of spiritual, energetic and psychological problems as and when they occur. This whole creation of ours is a very dynamic thing, and nothing stands still, which means that your human mechanism is essentially riding waves of existence from one point to another point. Maintaining perfect balance, stillness and calmness no matter what, is key to living beautifully. That is something only God can do.

GOD IS YOUR SERVANT

God isn't a higher level of intelligence than you, but in fact, a *lower* one. However, God lives in the details and it knows your being like no one else. Think about it this way: you may be the smartest person in your home or office, but you wouldn't simply step onto a train and try to run it, would you? It takes a lot of training just to do that, but now we're talking about your whole life experience. You, the spirit, simply are neither built for nor trained to run things at such a level of detail.

You weren't made to be in charge of your life. You do have the power to create, and set in motion a plan for your own life, which is exactly what all of you have done. But once the plan is set, you're expected to sit back, relax and enjoy the life you've already created as God takes the reins and runs it. It's like watching a movie: once the movie begins, you don't constantly muck around with the projection system, do you? But that is exactly what people have been trying to do for millennia, simply because they don't understand what God is doing and what you are supposed to be doing. More importantly, they simply don't understand that they aren't here to run things, but to simply enjoy things as they happen.

Life isn't about action, nor is it about studying, playing, working, etc. Life is fundamentally about simply experiencing whatever's going on. Each of us has decided to create an entirely different kind of life and experience it. We didn't come here to change how life goes, nor did we come here to put enormous amounts of effort into things like working. Each of us came here simply to experience a unique perspective on this infinite possibility we call life. Other than whatever the laws of existence prohibit, there is literally no limit to what kind of life one can experience, and humanity is capable of manifesting all of those possibilities. But look at the way most people live—their lives are indistinguishable from one another. At this point, the lives of most people in a developed country like the US contain only four things: working, eating, sleeping and entertainment (a great many things have become like "work" for people in the US, including childcare, exercise, etc.). This is simply due to the lack of understanding as to who we are and what we're here to do. Instead of using our full potential to enjoy a spectacular life that is totally unique, most of us are lost in the dull, drab slog of life that mostly involves mundane chores, unpleasant experiences and the same kinds of stuff that everyone else is also experiencing. Thanks to an obsession with action, the solution most people have come up with is to work harder at trying to create a better life, instead of what actually works—leaving it alone.

In the next chapter, I will explain why this has happened and why you start to fiddle with life instead of just allowing it to unfold as it should and accepting it for what it is, but for now, remember this much: God is your servant, interested in making sure your life goes perfectly. So don't pray to God, worship God, talk to God, etc. I have had "conversations" with many spiritual entities, but God is not one of them, because God doesn't speak at all! It is simply a very specific level of intelligence here to make things go well.

DON'T SURRENDER TO GOD

Out of this understanding that God is here to run things has come the idea that one must surrender oneself to God in order to live a good life. I've seen signs all across the country encouraging, goading, pleading with or threatening people to surrender to God. While the idea of surrendering to God is sound, in practice it is nearly impossible for most people to do, or more precisely, to endure. This is because God will always do the right thing for you whether you like it or not, and most of you cannot stand the way God works. Let me give you an example.

Let's say one fine morning you look at yourself in the mirror and see that you are fat. For most young people nowadays, being fat seems to be a real problem. It is true that many of you are, in fact, fatter than the previous generation used to be at your age. However, even though being fat has no effect on your life experience, worldly success or even true attraction, many of you have internalized a whole bunch of narratives about being fat that are all negative. And so it begins, a quest to "lose weight," "get in shape," etc. Now, depending on how you function, you may either try and hide the problem with clothing, try and change things using exercise and diet, use pharmaceuticals or take the surgical route. None of these things are God's way of fixing whatever it is you are dealing with.

First, God knows that being fat has nothing to do with being unhealthy, as some of you probably already know. God also knows that having a bad impression of yourself is, in fact, unhealthy. Instead of focusing on how your body looks, God will first look at whatever it is that is causing your body to go off kilter. Usually, this means going all the way down to your foundations (the energy layer), fixing whatever has gone wrong there and then—slowly—rebuilding the upper floors one by one. Not only is this process slow and laborious, it will also probably cause you to look *much worse* in the beginning and slowly get better, as God focuses on the deeper aspects first and the superficial aspects last. In other words, if you let God do the work, you will be healed from the inside out instead of simply being made to look better quickly.

But this is not what most of you want, at least at the layer that you are paying attention to, which is your thoughts and feelings. Thanks to the world in which you live, too many of you are addicted to taking control of little things in your life and tweaking things to make them exactly the way you want them, even if those "wants" are imposed upon you by the world, and not your own. Too many of you are dependent on things being fixed in your life as soon as they're broken and you refuse to wait and understand why they're broken. Too many of you care about the appearance of perfection as defined by the world around you, instead of actual health, wealth, wisdom and the like. So, if you surrender to God, and God starts to do things slowly and properly, you will have a nightmarish experience for a long time before you become wiser and see that everything is being done properly for a change.

In the past, many may have tried to convince you to surrender to God, but I am telling you simply: don't surrender to God. You don't know how anyway. Surrender should happen to you once your own intelligence has risen to the point where you understand why it is good for you, so we'll focus entirely on that. In other words, if surrender is necessary, it will happen because you allow it. That's all.

WHY IS GOD MISUNDERSTOOD?

The situation with every yogi, guru, saint and such is that we rarely sit down to write a book or make videos, as I have done. Most of my predecessors were content with sharing their power with the right people and enabling them to make great changes in the world, although most of their work is invisible and rarely acknowledged. As part of that, they shared wisdom with a few disciples who promptly misunderstood everything that was said. Most of the time these disciples didn't take good notes, if any. And often, those notes languished or were ignored. Then, many years (sometimes hundreds of years) later, people cobbled together a narrative based on some master's teachings and put together a textbook, scripture or something else. Often these books are a hodgepodge of narratives full of mistakes, omissions, misunderstandings, misinterpretations or worse, the disciples' own knowledge and discoveries!

In short, almost all the spiritual stuff you've read that isn't written by an enlightened being themselves, is garbage. And you shouldn't ever read it.

In almost every tradition, we have an entirely different kind of description of "God"; what "God" did, what "God" said, what "God" worked, and so on. Actually, the people who wrote this stuff were referring to multiple levels of intelligences operating in the universe, each of which does a specific kind of job, communicates in specific ways about specific things, guides beings in a unique manner, and so on. But these people weren't enlightened, and they had no understanding of what they were hearing or who they were hearing from (if they heard anything at all, i.e.).

The lesson for you is this: never listen to the talk of disciples, spiritual aspirants or people who haven't completed the journey. I have myself had the dubious privilege of being among groups of disciples (of other gurus) spewing nonsense like it was God's word. It is entertaining, to a point, but honestly, you are better off watching reality TV. A lot can happen while a human being is on the spiritual path, but clarity arrives only at the end. So, it's best if you stick to the teachings of a master if you can be 100% confident that no one else has messed with the narrative.

Or, find a *living* master and learn from them.

TIMES HAVE CHANGED

Of late, there have been some wonderful (legitimate) yogis, gurus and such who have made their teachings and Satsangs available online. You must be careful not to watch or listen to "remixes" of course, which are done by third parties who simply want to make a quick buck off the teachings of masters. Always go to the source for such things, which is why I am writing this book myself instead of giving the task to a gang of idiots and watching them make a mess of it. The yogis of the past didn't do what I am doing because some methods of communication simply weren't available, but there's another reason: things have changed.

There has been a big uptick in the level of energy that is available on this Earth. Do not think that the sudden shift we have made from being nomads, to being civilized, then suddenly becoming industrialized, and now putting Artificial Intelligence to work, is some sort of accident. The level of intelligence among human beings is rising, and (mostly subconsciously) human beings are starting to understand things about themselves they never understood before. This is the reason our young people are experiencing a full-blown identity crisis, along with its chief consequence—suicide. But what's important to know is that spiritually speaking, we no longer need the special techniques and Kriyas and meditations and yoga postures in order to get people to become enlightened. There is sufficient energy available now—thanks to the continuing evolution of our universe—for people to live normal lives and still arrive at enlightenment.

We are no longer in an age where yogis will primarily be found in the Himalayas, in caves, or in yoga centers. More and more you will find that yogis are like me—ordinary human beings living ordinary lives—but with enlightenment, wisdom and love to share. Of course, thanks to the Internet, you must be careful because there are now more false prophets around than ever before, but that is also the reason why I am writing this book as a guide. In the future, many of you must become enlightened and lead little groups of people here and there, instead of relying on a *system* such as a religion or a spiritual movement. In other words, humanity needs to bring spirituality down to Earth.

However, for this to happen, there needs to be another major shift in the way that human beings live, and this has to do with the biggest problem that all life has to contend with.

PAIN AND WHAT TO DO
ABOUT IT

Without exception, 100% of our civilization is a response to pain. At this point in our civilization, many people will disagree with this statement, because we have come up with many alternate, more comfortable ways of expressing the same idea. For instance, people may use the word *conservation* to justify planting more trees, the word *opportunity* to justify starting a new business, or even phrases like *improving quality of life* in order to justify the creation of a new medical procedure. But at the end of the day, all of it comes down to one thing and only one thing: we believe that not doing something will cause whatever it is we find painful to either continue or get worse and we don't want that. In other words, civilization is not only a response to pain, but is entirely about doing whatever we can to avoid pain.

If you didn't mind pain, you'd be happy to walk a few miles to the nearest river for water and wouldn't invent transportation or plumbing. If you didn't mind the rough ground, you'd go barefoot and wouldn't invent shoes, foot treatments or medication for cuts and bruises. If you didn't mind the heat and the bugs, you'd happily sleep under a tree and not invent air conditioning. If you didn't mind hunger, you'd wander until you found food instead of inventing agriculture. If you didn't mind the winds and the rains, you'd happily spend your days outside using the rocks, caves and trees for shelter, instead of inventing construction techniques.

And this situation continues today. If you didn't mind the pain, you would exercise a lot harder instead of looking for ways to avoid it, you'd give birth to a child without an epidural and allow your elderly to simply perish instead of propping them up with drugs and feeding tubes.

Most importantly, if you didn't mind pain, you would learn to love in the face of great obstacles instead of looking for a way out in every situation.

The American way of life (which is now almost universally adopted), is so allergic to pain, that we have built a world-wide economy focused totally on providing access to comfort, convenience and pleasure to varying degrees, all of which are designed to help you avoid or mask pain. And we've decided that we're better off accepting that other thing that happens when you reject pain and seek comfort, convenience and pleasure: suffering. But before we get to suffering, the question remains: why is there pain in the first place?

THE NATURE OF PAIN

Pain is simply the inability of life to flow freely. Recall the experience I shared with you in Chapter 2, where I said that Love is slowly dissolving all that exists into zero? Life, by nature, is limited, but what is beyond life is unlimited. Ultimately, life is trying to become *more* by giving itself up to a higher level of intelligence and becoming subtler in the process. Once something is subtler, it is a lot easier to work with, can flow freely and isn't impeded by anything in existence or beyond. To put it in terms of energy, information and intelligence, all forms of energy are trying to become more intelligent, and they can only do so by giving up information because having less information is what makes anything less rigid and subtler. The subtler something is, the freer it is. The subtler something is, the more intelligently it can respond to everything.

For example, take a rock. A rock has a lot of rigidity in it, which is to say, it has a lot of information. A rock simply refuses to yield, to flex and to bend around situations—all of which are abilities granted by intelligence.

As a consequence, a rock is impeded everywhere and itself acts as an impediment to other things. You'll find that in our world, people who are full of information such as ideas, beliefs and preconceived notions act exactly this way. They are impeded everywhere they go and they impede others trying to get on with their lives.

Water, which is subtler, isn't impeded in general as it can find a way around most situations, but it too sometimes finds obstacles that cannot be overcome easily (e.g. a dam). Then comes air, which is nearly impossible to impede as it can find the tiniest little opening to seep through. This continues, until we get to the spirit, which is totally impossible to impede because it is the subtlest of all. It passes through and flows freely no matter what's in the way. There are absolutely no limits or bounds on the spirit—even the laws of existence don't apply—which means that in the world of spirit you can *literally* do anything.

Now, everything in existence is trying to become *spiritual*, which is to say, trying to become as subtle as possible and as intelligent as possible, so that it too can flow freely. This is where pain comes in. Whatever wants to become spiritual must be willing to go through a process through which it gives up information (i.e., its structure, its rigidity) and becomes a lot subtler. If that something is *willing* to give up information, it will not experience pain, but if it isn't willing, and must be forced in some way, it experiences pain. In other words, anything that impedes the release of information by resisting the natural tendency of all life to become spiritual experiences pain. There is nothing you or I can do about it.

You can argue with God (who won't respond), or with any other level of intelligence in the universe about the way that life is made, but no one's going to change it, because it is just the way life is made! You know, what we're all experiencing isn't the first-time creation has happened, nor will it necessarily be the last. Each time creation happens, things are different. But in *this* creation cycle, this is the way things are. You can accept them as they are, or suffer and lament at the way life is made. Either way, pain is here, it's real and you must experience it, even if to a lesser degree than say, a rock does, or an animal.

Oh yes! Something that is physical experiences a lot more pain than you do. We, as human beings, are blessed with the ability to transform pain and release it in all sorts of ways, but lower levels of beings (i.e., less spiritual ones) just don't have that kind of ability. This is why animals don't heal from traumas as well as human beings can, and the reason why, if you're going to inflict pain on an animal, you must kill it and eat it so that you carry whatever suffering the animal may have endured. Don't torture anything in existence, especially an animal. Don't kill animals for sport. Treating a lower level of intelligence poorly will backfire on you very badly, and since you are, in fact, the highest possible level of intelligence there is, if you treat *anything* poorly (even a piece of clothing), your life will take a turn for the worse.

But given that we are exalted beings in some ways and are blessed with many abilities that less spiritual entities aren't, is there a way out of pain? In other words, is pain necessary?

IS PAIN NECESSARY?

No! Pain is *not* necessary, at least not forever. It *is* possible to live without pain even as human beings—for the most part. As long as there is a physical body, it is not possible to get rid of pain 100%, because physicality implies rigidity to some extent, but if you go through the spiritual enlightenment process, you will find that the pain in your whole life is minimized to a point where you never pay attention to it, never care about it and never do anything about it either.

For example, I don't bother with whatever pain comes into my body once in a while. I am not allowed to go to the doctor anyway, not because I choose not to, but because there is a higher level of intelligence guiding me that makes it so. Regardless, I have absolutely no interest in taking care of whatever pain there is. My experience of life is focused entirely on love, to be totally honest with you. Whatever I do, all I experience is a great love, which is like a warm current of ecstasy flowing through me so I don't pay attention to anything else. Let me give you an example.

Many people like to lift heavy weights in the gym and I am one of them. I push harder and harder every day—not by force, but by nature—because I am getting stronger every day, and my body simply responds by accepting heavier weights every day without complaining. People who lift heavy weights will tell you that they must overcome a pain barrier in order to really grow big muscles, but my experience of working out isn't at all like that. I always work out to the point of *failure*, i.e., to the point where my muscles simply cannot lift any more weight. When I experience failure, it is simply that—a failure. My body fails without pain, no matter what I do. It simply goes as far as it can go and stops. In other words, when I push hard, at some point my body simply yields and falls apart without resisting, causing me no pain whatsoever.

This is something that I hope many of you can experience: a life without pain, for the most part, which is possible only when you're enlightened. It's not that my body is numb or insensitive. It's just got very little in the way of structure actually holding it together, meaning that I am actually quite fragile physically even though I don't look like it. But it's a kind of flexible fragility, in the sense that when I have an accident, for example, my body simply yields and falls apart and then is put back together. Unlike most people I know, it doesn't break. Let me share with you another story to illustrate.

AN ACCIDENT

After the end of my healing period, I spent about 2 years traveling the United States, speaking to many young women and observing their inner world. The last of these 2 years was spent in the city of Los Angeles, which, in my view, is spiritually the darkest place on Earth. I was asked (by the Divine Feminine) to write a blog targeted towards teenage women in Los Angeles so I could come to terms with the level of corruption facing society. This is because women always lead the charge in society no matter what is going on. I will say more about this later.

When I arrived in Los Angeles after a year of riding my motorcycle around the country, I was actually in a very bad state because of just how much suffering I had witnessed among the young women I had met. So, while I was in LA, I would walk at least 5-6 hours a day, swim as often as possible in the ocean, bicycle around and most importantly, ride my motorcycle on the weekends in the isolation of the Verdugo mountains in the fresher, cleaner air just to keep myself healthy. Despite my best efforts though, I was unable to release all the pain I was accumulating thanks to living near downtown LA and experiencing all of its decrepitude, its filth and its darkness. When this happens, life sometimes intervenes in order to help you release a whole lot of pain at once. This is what people call "an accident."

One Sunday morning, after having ridden for about 2 hours, my motorcycle's brakes gave way, and I crashed head on onto the wall of a canyon at 55 miles an hour. My bike disintegrated and was a total loss, as they say. I was thrown off the bike, tumbled over some jagged rocks and came to rest face down and unconscious by the side of the road. Some good Samaritans found me and arranged for me to be transported down the mountain and eventually I found myself in the emergency room in a nearby hospital.

There's a lot more to this story, but here's what happened to my body: nothing. The nurse at the emergency room sent me to the X-ray room twice because they didn't understand why nothing was broken. My helmet was smashed, my bike was a total wreck (even the fuel tank was busted and leaking fuel), but here I was, with barely a scratch despite being dressed in a T-shirt, jeans and tennis shoes.

This is what happens if your body simply gives in to whatever is going on. Some people call this kind of thing "luck," but I've had 12 motorcycle accidents (the others weren't as bad) and never broken a single bone. In addition, I've had many accidents, fallen many times in ice, crashed a mountain bike into a ravine and broken the bike, tumbled down slopes into welcoming cacti—you name it. In every case, I simply got up and walked off. In every case, all that happened was that I experienced a huge amount of pain leaving me, and that was it.

If I step on a sharp rock I experience pain, but my experience of pain is simply just another experience and doesn't cause any problems. In fact, I enjoy pain because it's so rare, and because it affects me so deeply, even if only for a split second. I can feel the pain percolating all the way into the depths of my being and not simply remaining on the surface. And because

I am touched so deeply by it, whenever I do experience it, my body breaks out into a big smile and starts laughing. I cannot explain it. It's almost like I've met a familiar friend again.

The flip side to the way my body works is that because it so easily and quickly releases all the pain it accumulates, it also releases as much energy as is needed to get rid of the pain. This means that over time, I've gotten very thin, spiritually speaking. One more serious illness, a serious accident, or even a negative encounter with a human being in the world is enough to kill me. In other words, because of the way my body is made, its grip on life is very loose. All animals live this way—they're very easy to kill.

To give you an analogy, I am like a very big, but very thin balloon. I can hold enormous amounts of energy, but I can be popped easily, instantly turning into nothing. I am telling you all this because if you walk the path of light and become enlightened, you will also be like me. You will not be "tough," but gentle and vulnerable and you will be easy to destroy.

If this is the case, how have I survived even this long? Truth be told, I've been literally living on borrowed Time and energy. The work I did in the past allows me to receive energy from people I don't even know, and they've been sustaining me for a while now. It is entirely life's decision as to how long this state of affairs will continue, which is why I've always told people that I am being kept alive for something.

So, the consequence of not holding onto pain is that you become easy to kill and exist entirely at the mercy of the world around you. But whatever else may be said about pain, one thing is certain: pain is enormously beneficial, and everyone should welcome it. Do not go seeking pain, inflicting pain on yourself or on others, but welcome it if it arrives uninvited. The reason for this lies in the way human experience works.

THE NATURE OF EXPERIENCE

Whatever you experience in life, you do so when it is leaving you, for good. This is true of pain, pleasure, distress, anxiety, indeed everything. Far from being something that is imposed upon you by outside forces, your experience of life starts deep inside you and slowly proceeds to the outside. This means that your experience of life actually begins in the realm of the spirit, becomes manifest in the realm of energy and then finally becomes apparent in the realm of physicality. However, there are some things you haven't created that you will experience because your body is trying to get rid of them and pain is one of those things. When I lived in Los Angeles, I did not create the pain I was experiencing, but I absorbed it from the people around me. When I released all that pain, I experienced something that I hadn't created for myself. Let me give you another example to illustrate this important point.

Let's say it's a beautiful sunny day, the weather is nice and you are outside enjoying an ice cream cone. This specific experience is something you wanted and created for yourself so you could enjoy it. The nature of this experience and how much you are enjoying it actually has nothing to do with the Sun, the weather or the ice cream. These things are "scenery" and they can change depending on where the world is at any given moment. You can have a beautiful experience of life eating an ice cream cone in the sun, or while reading a book in a quiet library, or simply sitting at home. You can have a beautiful experience of life being a Greek on some remote island in the Mediterranean a thousand years ago, or being lost in a virtual reality app inside your cramped apartment. The scenery around you has everything to do with the way the world is, and very little to do with your actual experience of life. When your body is in perfect condition, it creates only good experiences no matter what the scenery looks like. This is true because none of us actually came here to experience a bad life. You, the spirit, are too intelligent to have created a stupid, worthless and miserable life and live it out. So, in your normal state, you only experience life as being amazing and beautiful, all the time.

Regardless of the scenery, let's say someone walks by and starts cursing at you and throwing objects in your face. Suddenly, your experience of life will not be as beautiful. This again, has little to do with the way the world is and everything to do with what your body does when something "bad" is happening. When someone starts to curse at you or throw things at you, it's not important what they are saying or throwing. What matters is the energy they are casting in your direction. If the energy they are throwing at you is good, i.e., it is pure, you'll feel uplifted, happy even. This happens often when a dog shows up and goes crazy with excitement, rubbing against you, licking you, etc. The energy of every other creature except human beings is usually pure and most people don't mind being covered in it at all—in fact they start laughing and playing with the dog, cat or even a lizard. But if you encounter a negative human being who's yelling and screaming and throwing even a blade of grass in your direction, you'll feel sick.

This feeling of sickness has to do with the fact that your body is trying desperately to get rid of the impurity in the energy being thrown at you. In other words, you are being given some tainted energy, but your body wants pure energy with nothing attached. Impurity in the energy you receive is always in the form of bad information, so your body will start throwing out all the bad information from the energy you received as quickly as possible. And this experience—of bad information leaving you—is what you'll experience as negativity, i.e., negative thoughts, negative feelings and so on. There are limits to how fast your body can process the bad information you're receiving and throw it out, especially if your body is too tired or sick. If you receive too much bad information at once, you'll absorb all of it and not be able to release the bad information quickly enough. You may wait a long time (sometimes decades) before that bad information comes out, which happens a lot to people. In my case in Los Angeles, it took a year and some months before my body was able to finally kick out all of the impurity I had accumulated while traveling across the US. Regardless, whenever bad information leaves you, you will feel sick.

This is exactly what's going on whenever you experience pain. Something or the other has entered your system that is causing you to *resist* the changes life is bringing, even if only subconsciously. Once the pain leaves you, it means that whatever was resisting has yielded. This mechanism by which you internalize something that makes you resist life can occur at every layer in the body. You may resist things psychologically, physically and energetically. Depending on which layer is being affected, the pain will be more or less severe.

WHY YOU RESIST LIFE

As I've described to you, most of you don't like the idea that life is about experiencing something, giving it up and moving forward because most of you like to hold on to things. As Love slowly dissolves all that exists, things, people and situations in your life will slowly fall apart and disappear. The more you resist this process, the more pain you will feel and the more you will want to hold on to whatever you already have, because you incorrectly believe that pain is a bad thing. In other words, when you experience pain, you hold on to things even more tightly in hopes that you can "defeat" the process of life, in some way. You don't just hold on to things at the psychological layer, but at every layer in the body. For instance, many people experience a lot of body fat that simply refuses to leave—this has everything to do with something deeper in the body holding on to that fat and not wanting to let it go. And this act of holding on to things, people and situations is a direct reaction to pain.

Since childhood, you were taught that pain is a bad thing, that it means something is wrong and that you should seek help and do something in order to make sure the pain is "gone." Instead of being told the truth about pain and that it is good for you, you were convinced that you needed to do something to fix it. Now, remember you experience something when it's leaving you. So, if you're trying not to experience pain, it means you are trying to prevent pain from leaving you. In other words, trying to "fix" the pain basically means doing just about everything you can to *not* experience it, aka suppression.

This is the way of darkness and the way of the world in general. The world is constantly coming up with narratives as to why pain is a bad thing, why it must not be experienced, why it must be suppressed, treated, fixed, etc. Are you at all surprised that we have an epidemic of escapism going on? People are trying desperately to escape from the reality that pain is here and that it must be experienced in order for us to be healthy. And so, we have untold number of strategies available at this point for people to try and escape or suppress their experience of pain: entertainment, pharmaceuticals and procedures, even some naturopathic "treatments," alcohol and hard drugs (e.g., fentanyl) and finally, suicide.

Unfortunately, none of these strategies work, because of the way Time works, which is the focus of the next chapter.

PAIN MUST BE ENDURED

Ultimately, the only way to be free of pain is to release the pain that is already inside your system. If you don't do that, you will never be free of the pain that is natural to living in a civilization that has done everything possible to prevent you from experiencing it. Do not think that avoiding pain while you are alive will somehow allow you to cheat and get away with not experiencing it. At some point in your life (or after death), you will have to experience every ounce of pain you have accumulated as it leaves you. Let me share with you another experience I had to illustrate.

On a silent Christmas night, I was sitting in my home in North Carolina alone. The wife and family were still at her parents' home catching up. I had come home because I was feeling really strange inside and just needed to be alone in a pure environment for a bit. I was sitting in the dark next to a Christmas tree lit up with blinking lights of many colors. The Moon was bright and its light was streaming in through the south-facing windows. Everything was at peace—on the outside.

As I sat there, I felt something rising from very deep inside me—a kind of feeling that I didn't know I could experience at such depths in my body. It was deeper than my bones and seemed to be at the energy layer. As I sat there, this feeling overwhelmed me and I had no choice but to keep quiet and wait. A minute passed and it became clear to me that this "feeling" was pain: pure, unadulterated pain the likes of which I had never felt before. The pain slowly started to spread all over my body and in a matter of minutes, completely enveloped me.

Have you ever eaten a dinner roll? You know, those little pieces of bread sometimes served in a basket at the table? If you've ever had one of those, you know what you do with them is use both your hands to pull that piece of bread apart and eat it. When you're pulling it apart, you can see every little strand and fiber of bread stretching and tearing until the two pieces separate. *That* is how this pain felt, except it was as if every cell in my body was being torn and re-torn endlessly. I don't have words for what I experienced that night, because these "cells" weren't just at the physical layer, but also deeper down, at an energy layer. It's as if everything that was existential about me, i.e., everything that wasn't spiritual, was being remade by tearing it apart and putting it back together over and over.

The pain was so unbelievable that it made me go completely silent and numb in a way. I cannot describe the pain as being excruciating, because in fact I've had an experience where I sat on my couch and experienced the crucifixion of Jesus within me. *That* was excruciating, but *this* was at a whole different level. And it continued on and on for a good hour or so. After a point, the pain started to slowly subside and I drove back to the family gathering where I paced back and forth as the last vestiges of pain dissipated.

All that pain was what I had taken on during my years of working spiritually among women. I had taken on their insecurities, their insanity, their suffering—whatever they threw at me really—and I hadn't had a chance to heal from it during the first 33 years of my life. Finally, one fine day my body decided it was a good time to release it all, so it did, with zero warning.

I am fortunate in that I had time to heal from my work and experience the release of all this pain before death, but most people never give themselves the chance to do so. What I experienced was not just physical pain, but also energetic pain. Energetic pain is what you'll experience after you die, if you don't experience all the pain you were supposed to while you were alive. If you don't want to go through what I did, then allow yourself to experience and release pain as soon as it appears. Do not suppress it with drugs, nor go to the doctor for treatments. The only problem with this advice is that sometimes, whatever is causing the pain will kill you if you don't get treatment and it is for this reason that I will let you decide what it is you want to do.

However, even if you do get treatment, the pain associated with whatever was causing issues in the first place will have to be experienced by you *at some point*, either while you are alive, or while you are dead.

In other words, whatever it is you came here to experience, or picked up along the way, you *must* experience fully before you are totally finished. No amount of medical intervention will save you from having to experience life, because of how Time works.

TIME AND DEATH

AN EXPERIENCE OF TIME

On a Fall morning in Raleigh, North Carolina, I walked like I did on most Fridays to a conference room with my manager to have our weekly 1-on-1 sessions, a chance for me to discuss how things were going, receive suggestions and get the scoop on whatever was going on in the rest of the company I was working in. The work I was doing on the surface was like the work any other Product Manager did and there wasn't anything challenging about it. However, on the inside, known only to a couple of people with whom I regularly shared descriptions of my experiences and insights, I was having a series of spiritual experiences on an almost daily basis. These experiences would come on around 11 AM like clockwork and dissipate in about 30 minutes, followed by a whole series of insights that would pour into me throughout the day and well into the next morning. It was exhausting, but also incredibly enriching and beautiful, as I was often given direct experiences of things that I had only heard people talk about.

On this particular day though, my meeting was at 9 AM and as soon as my manager and I sat down, I knew something was going to happen. Within seconds, I felt transported into a different dimension in addition to the one I was in, where I perceived things were no longer linear. As my manager spoke, I began to perceive that his words were starting in a dimension outside of my experience, emerging into my experience and falling inward into a central "hole," like a vortex of some sort. Now, whenever I would have a spiritual experience, by its very nature I would lose all control over my body and turn into a pure witness, watching everything happen by itself. And so it was that in addition to my manager's words that the words coming out of my body also started to do the same thing. This phenomenon soon spread to everything in my awareness. Everything in the meeting room, including the furniture, the lighting and the notebook in front of me, was in one dimension exactly where they always were, but in another dimension emerging out of nowhere, and falling into the vortex in the center, over and over.

Initially, I thought this was amusing. I had always known that our physical reality is a matter of perception and that there is no such thing as a "chair," for example. There is only energy, intelligence and information and however our bodies (themselves a combination of those three things) interpret them. But pretty soon, this phenomenon crossed over into the realm of psychology as well, and not only the words, but even the meaning and the very sounds making up those words were soon all emerging out of nowhere and falling into the vortex.

Now this wasn't easy to endure, because all of a sudden, I had full awareness of what was going on without being able to make sure that the words coming out of the mouth of my body made any sense. It was as if everything was simply created out of energy, manifesting and unmanifesting, all in one timeless moment. This continued on for 30 minutes—as long as the meeting lasted actually—and afterwards, slowly dissipated over the course of a minute or so. I heaved a sigh of relief, took a bit to relax (these experiences would take every ounce of energy I had) and got back to my normal schedule.

What I had experienced was how Time works.

A LITTLE BIT OF UNDERSTANDING

Time is really intricate, and its functioning is so integral to our experience of life as human beings that none of us will be given full insight into how it works. Nor would I advise you to try to unlock its mysteries, because if you did understand Time, you would perish instantly. There is no way to remain alive in a human body once the illusion of Time itself is stripped away. So, I will not give you a full understanding of how Time works, nor can I. I will only share with you a little bit, just enough so that you understand why your life is going the way it is.

First of all, Time isn't "real." It's just another dimension of experience (and there are many of them—28 by my count so far!). We, as the spirit, obviously pervade all dimensions at once, but as human beings, we are only experiencing one of these dimensions. If you are reading this book like normal human beings do (as opposed to experiencing it in another dimension), you are essentially experiencing the Time dimension.

While scientists continue to believe that things like space, time and gravity are real, all yogis know these are simply experiences. In fact, space is made possible as an experience only in the Time dimension, while gravity, well, there's no such thing actually. Regardless, if you build an instrument to observe a certain kind of effect, then you will definitely measure it in some way. That doesn't make it real, but I digress.

Time has a specific property, in that it can either move forward, slow down or stop, but cannot go backwards in existence. You *can* read Time backwards and forwards if you go beyond Time into the realm of the spirit, but these are things few yogis have ever done and it's not important for you to experience. You can think of Time essentially as a spiral that has a definite beginning—for you—and a definite end—again, for you. On this spiral are experiences that you've decided you want to have in this lifetime, so to speak. As your body "travels" through Time, it is basically Time that is slowly spiraling, "unraveling," or "unfolding" so that you experience one situation after another. Some yogis in the past have described this as the "reel of Time," as if Time is like a movie reel: a spiral slowly unraveling. But there is something special about this unraveling: the spiral can get "stuck," in the sense that instead of spiraling and unraveling, it is possible that time stops. When this happens, you experience the same situations over and over as if you are stuck in a cycle.

The reason I am saying this can happen to you, specifically, is because Time isn't exactly "shared." Yes, we all share *an* experience of Time and yes, Time works the same way for all of us, but *your* Time and *my* Time are not at all the same. They are, in fact, separate spirals. Your time unravels at whatever speed you allow it to, while my Time unravels at whatever speed I allow it to. There is absolutely nothing in common between your Time and my Time. It is as if we are both watching our own movie reels, *except* all the reels are superimposed on one screen.

This is how our universe works. Every intelligent creature (plant, animal, even rock, or planet) is projecting its own movie reel and when it's all put together, we see what we call "reality." Actually, what most people call "reality," i.e., the sensory reality, is anything but real. If it were, in fact, real, we wouldn't have people (yogis and the mentally ill alike!) experiencing things outside physical reality. Reality isn't negotiable, but our physical reality, which consists of what we see, taste, touch, hear, smell and feel, is entirely a product of Time and perception and is therefore, easily changed.

By the way, next time you look at your watch, or your phone and see it ticking away, understand that that number has absolutely nothing to do with Time and everything to do with the rate of expenditure of energy. If our planet were given a boost of energy, our days would suddenly be less than 24 hours long. This goes for our solar system, the galaxy and even the universe. The measurement of Time, as it is popularly understood, is bogus—just another narrative that you should consider little more than entertainment and not worry about. This also means that your "age," as defined by the number of Earth years passed, is totally meaningless. If you had the energy of a 10-year-old, you might well be able to live life like a 10-year-old even at 90 years of age—and there are some who do. I, for instance, have always felt like a teenager around 17 years of age. This hasn't changed with age, or Time.

WHY TIME STOPS

Like a river, Time wants to flow unimpeded, but there is something interesting about how our life unfolds on this Earth that you must understand. Life *insists* that you experience everything that you set out to experience, and experience it *thoroughly*. It really cares that every single detail that you wanted be given to you. I am not talking about just people, things and situations, but even the smallest little detail—such as the angle at which your phone is lying next to you. Every step and every breath is calibrated perfectly to you and everything is made the way you wanted it to be. So, when people complain that their life isn't perfect, I tell you, they have no one to blame but themselves.

The problem for most people is that life insists that you experience *everything* thoroughly, i.e., not just pleasure, for example, but also pain. As I've shared with you in the last chapter, pain is a natural part of living on this Earth and life insists that you experience all the pain that you are given fully with your eyes wide open, alert and aware. Depending on what kind of life you came here to live through, you may have to experience a little bit of pain or a lot. In my case, I was asked to serve spiritually, so at least the first 42 years of my life were filled with enormous amounts of pain I took on from other people, released, then took on some more and so on. If you came here to live a quiet, simple life in the country, for example, you may not have to experience all that, but you will have more pain of a different kind—things like heat and cold, cuts and scrapes, insects and animals, etc.

What's happening with most of you is that when you don't like something, you immediately turn away from it instead of becoming willing to experience it, nonetheless. Being willing to experience life is what many people call "acceptance," but acceptance isn't a concept. Acceptance is a way of life. Acceptance means that you are willing to experience life as it comes, even if it kills you, maims you, leaves you disabled, whatever.

Don't misunderstand me. I am not talking about jumping off a bridge into a river just because your friends dared you to do so, taking heroin because your classmates goaded you into it, or getting into the pornography industry because everyone in your social network insists you must try it at least once. None of those things count as acceptance, but they may count as stupidity. What I am talking about is accepting the life that you came here to live, which has absolutely *nothing* to do with what other people say or ask or want you to do.

Read that last sentence again, carefully, if you didn't get it. Your life has absolutely *nothing* to do with other people. You have no responsibilities, no obligation towards others and nothing to gain from others. You are not required to even pay attention to anyone or anything else other than your life, period. *However*, if others do throw things at you, physically coerce you or somehow trick you into doing something that isn't good for you, you must accept it, endure it and shut up, because *that* is, in fact, something you arranged for yourself, either on purpose or by mistake.

So, let's say you get pulled over by the cops and they—wrongly—detain you, accuse you of something you didn't do and punish you. Walking the path of light requires that you shut up and take it. Otherwise, you are essentially refusing to accept what life is throwing at you. I will explain in the next chapter why this kind of thing is happening to so many people, and may have happened to you as well, but there are no ifs and buts when it comes to accepting life as it comes. You must accept it all.

This is something Jesus tried to tell you, by the way. He even tried to show you what acceptance means using His own life example. But you didn't listen and decided He was doing what He did in order to save you. He wasn't. I'll tell you what He actually was doing later in this book.

Coming back to Time though, what happens when you don't accept everything with open arms? Time stops.

MOVING FORWARD REQUIRES TOTAL ACCEPTANCE

There are a lot of people on the planet nowadays that are out on the streets protesting, complaining and asking for things to change. In addition to wasting all their resources and in fact, making things worse in a way, most of these people are essentially putting a stop to Time in their own lives. When you refuse to accept your life as it is, Time comes to a standstill and you will essentially go into a cycle, repeating the same experiences over and over and over again. As I've said before, as Time passes for other creatures, the *scenery* on Earth will change, because they are moving forward in their own lives. And there are a fair number of people who are somewhat slowly but surely accepting whatever is being thrown at them, meaning that Time is moving forward for them as well. However, *essentially*, your life will remain exactly the same, from one year to the next, from one decade to the next and even from one lifetime to the next.

In fact, most people on this Earth haven't moved forward in a very long time! Thousands of years ago, human beings were running around on foot trying to fulfill desires they didn't realize weren't theirs but were given to them by someone else. Now they are running around in electric cars, trying to fulfill desires given to them via TV or social media. Essentially, life hasn't actually moved forward on this Earth at all, not for most people. If it had, most of you would be yogis, experiencing all the cool stuff happening in the rest of the universe and beyond.

If you want to move forward in life and experience everything that you yourself set out to experience, you must accept life as it comes and not resist a single thing. However, here comes the first big difference between the men and the women: women *can* and *must* refuse to accept whatever it is they don't want in their lives.

EXCEPT IN THE CASE OF WOMEN

In Volume II, there is an entire chapter on femininity and the difference it makes as far as life on Earth is concerned, because the way a woman is expected to live her life on this Earth is *drastically* different from how a man is expected to live his life. This is something that women haven't ever accepted, understood or even tried to learn, but this is why I am here and why I was put through so much trouble with women—so that I could share those insights with you. Later on, when I outline some practical tips on helping you progress, I will clearly separate guidance for men and women, because it is not the same, it cannot be the same and it will never be the same in this creation cycle.

For now, women need to understand this: you, as a woman, must *silently* refuse to accept whatever it is you don't want. Don't go out and protest, don't fight, don't argue, don't complain and certainly don't waste energy trying to change anything. However, while a man must accept whatever the hell he is given, you, as a woman, must only accept whatever it is you *really* want. Unfortunately, most women have no idea what they really want and their idea of what they want is defined more and more by the society in which they live, This means that when it comes to understanding what to accept and how to accept it, the vast majority of women will utterly fail to do the right thing and get into boatloads of trouble, which is exactly where all our young women are headed. Until a woman is enlightened, she will have absolutely no idea what she really wants in life, which is why in later chapters I go into so much detail on how to make sure that you, as a woman, give yourself the best chance of becoming enlightened.

But coming back to Time, in general, what happens when Time stops? Do you get to live the same life forever? No, because at some point, your energy will come to an end. This is one of the ways in which you will die.

DEATH

The amount of energy and Time you are given, is limited. You don't get more energy by eating food, sitting in the sun or sucking the life out of other people. You *can* make the body last longer by doing those things, but even in the case of food, specifically, you need energy to digest it, which means that at some point you'll run out of energy and lose interest in eating, as many elderly people do.

If you run out of Time or energy, or both, you will die. You can also end the physical body by other means such as accidents and suicide, for example. However, your physical body is merely a thin veneer on top of your energy, which you cannot kill by any means.

This, by the way, is why suicide doesn't work. You, as a human being, simply don't have the power to destroy energy. All you can do, at best, is cause harm to, or end the physical body in some way. The energy behind the physical body will not die and if it has Time left, it will simply put on new clothing, so to speak, and enter this dimension once more (assuming a womb is available to give birth to it). This simple phenomenon is what some people are blowing out of proportion and calling "reincarnation" and such, but it's just the first law of thermodynamics in action, to be honest!

By the way, this is also the reason you are not going to find any ghosts or spirits opening doors, making noises, possessing people or whatever nonsense you've seen, heard or read about. You have to be in the Time dimension to affect the Time dimension and you can only be here if you are embodied. All those people who experienced beings coming to them and such were experiencing a higher dimension, not "ghosts."

Regardless, the only way you'll really understand the truth about death is by experiencing it, which is anyway guaranteed. Good for you.

But I want to give you a rudimentary understanding of what happens if you don't accept life as it comes, don't live the life you really want, refuse to accept pain and either impede or stop the flow of Time in your life. Once your physical body is gone, the rest of whatever is there, is no longer bound by Time, which means you will go through every single experience you haven't already gone through, including all the pain and pleasure you were supposed to go through, *instantly.* Some people have referred to this phenomenon as "your life flashing before your eyes," but that is only partially true. What will happen is that all of your life experience, including whatever you hadn't experienced, will flash before you.

Understand that everything you're experiencing in the physical dimension is essentially a matter of Time and perception, and not real. This means that all of your beliefs, memories, relationships, possessions, indeed everything that you are holding on to in some way, is just an experience you are having in Time. There are no relatives waiting for you, nor is there anyone in particular interested in meeting you after death. You don't get to meet Jesus or Krishna or anyone in particular simply because you believe in them. If you had, in fact, lived the life you wanted and Time came to an end for you *before* your energy came to an end, then you may experience a different dimension of existence where there are levels of intelligences you may recognize as Jesus, a saint that walked the Earth at some point, a guru you knew or Krishna, etc. This is what some people are calling heaven.

But for most people on this Earth, including all of you who either slowed down or stopped Time by refusing to accept your life, you will be alone after death. In this state, as your whole life flashes before you, you will experience pain, suffering, regret, grief, loss, negativity and so on as you realize that you wasted the only chance you had at experiencing a beautiful life. Since your body at this point is not bound by Time, you will more or less "explode" because your physical body in the Time dimension was the only thing limiting the bounds of or the speed at which you could experience things.

In other words, you will experience limitless suffering, which is what some people are calling hell. And since this suffering is outside the Time dimension, it is "eternal." Hence the term: eternal hell.

ETERNITY

Do not confuse eternity to mean "forever." Eternity simply means "beyond Time." Eternal heaven or hell doesn't last "forever," because there is no "forever" outside Time. It is simply a question of energy dissipating as a consequence of Love consuming all.

People like me, who have done the hard spiritual work and transformed ourselves, don't experience Time at all. In my life, everything simply happens. In fact, I don't really experience anything in the traditional sense anymore, which is to say that I am done having experiences and don't have any use for them. There is only energy surging at times, which is why I said that pain makes no difference—it is just another surge of energy and does not bring up any problems. If you live like this, you are essentially living beyond Time, which some people are calling eternal life. In other words, eternal life is an experience you're expected to have while on this Earth and not only after you die.

DOWN TO EARTH

All these highfalutin spiritual ideas are of no use to those of you who don't even clearly see what it is that you want to do every moment of your life, but they have caused a lot of confusion and made people believe in very many nonsensical things. I know millions of people that are struggling to become enlightened, find peace, overcome suffering, find release from pain and so on that are all doing the wrong thing such as meditating, praying, going to a religious institution or hoping a guru will simply give them a handout. All of these techniques are wrong, because they were never intended to do all that people are hoping they would do. Gurus gave specific practices to specific disciples in order to unburden them from specific beliefs, lifestyles, addictions, misunderstandings and so on, but these things have taken on a life of their own and lost all meaning. I've come across books about yoga, meditation and even "spirituality" written by total idiots passing themselves off as experts on the subject. And it seems just about anyone with exceptional bodily flexibility is teaching a yoga class nowadays.

It is time that we give up all of these useless practices and come back down to Earth. Enlightenment, which is a prerequisite to total peace, wisdom, understanding, true wealth, unbridled happiness, satisfaction, fulfillment and the ability to create a beautiful life, is a consequence of true living, hard work in the face of tremendous obstacles and real courage. This was the case for the Buddha, for Jesus, for Sri Ramana Maharshi, for Sri Nisargadatta Maharaj, for Sadhguru, for millions of yogis who have come and gone, and it has been the case for me. Everything else that happened along the way is a side effect at best, not the cause of enlightenment.

You don't have to run into the woods like some of those yogis did, nor do you have to starve in the desert, but you must be willing to accept life and move forward. This takes intelligence, and you must grow in intelligence every moment of your life if you really want to make it. The best part about living in our universe is that your intelligence is naturally wanting to grow every moment. All you have to do is get out of the way and not make things harder for yourself. But this is easier done than said!

Yes, in fact, all these tips that I am going to share with you in the coming chapters are really easy to put into practice and a lot harder to explain, which is why it's taken me so long to find the right words. And this is why I am inviting every *worthy* young woman to consider living with me because I could just show you how to be instead of having to explain every little detail. However, for the sake of the billions that are simply not qualified (for example, among the billions of women walking this Earth, I expect no more than *one* to succeed on this path in my lifetime, and that is enough), I am going to describe in as much detail as I can what you, the young people of the world, can do in order to ensure that you raise your intelligence and keep it growing as long as you live, until you yourself arrive at the point of enlightenment.

COMMITMENT

The tips and practices I cover in Volume II—not yogic practices but natural ones, like bathing properly—are going to require a change of lifestyle at some point. While the path of light is open to you no matter where you are today, do not expect that you can continue killing people for a living, work in the pornographic industry or exploit people's ignorance in order to make money—just to name a few examples—and expect to get to the end. This has absolutely nothing to do with societal expectations or morality and everything to do with making sure you are in the best environment for your intelligence to grow. You must and will become a human being whose footprint on this Earth is minimized, while your positive impact is maximized. As you read this book, you will know why that matters, and why that will happen automatically.

I am not one to mince words with people, not even in real life. I am the kind of yogi that tells people to their face that they are incredibly beautiful and really need to care about their life, or that they have no chance of succeeding in this lifetime or that the best they can expect is to be happy on their deathbed and no sooner. So, I am telling you this straight up: walking the path of light is the hardest thing you will ever do, *if* you aren't totally committed. If you are totally committed, you will still struggle, but you will pull through. Regardless, as long as you are on the way, life isn't going to be a cakewalk. You must be fierce at some level in order to succeed, but everything you need, even courage and ferocity, will come to you as and when you really need it.

We are not alone. There are millions of forces and many levels of intelligences *actively* collaborating to ensure that those of you who are committed succeed, and succeed in this lifetime. But *they* are going to succeed only to the extent that *you* are committed. Do not think of these forces and beings as people cheering for you—they are simply sources of wisdom, guidance, intelligence and whatever else you need. Open yourself to life and they will flow into you, making your progress smoother, that's all.

So, take a deep breath, put this book away for a while, and when you're ready to really commit to the path of light right from Day One for the rest of your life, start reading Volume II.

VOLUME II

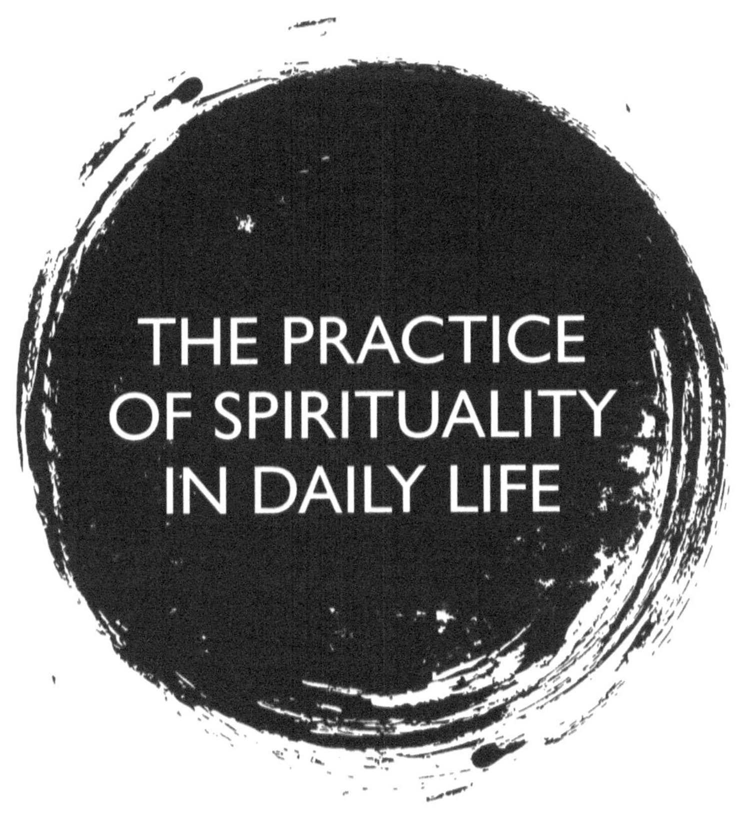

THE PRACTICE
OF SPIRITUALITY
IN DAILY LIFE

BAD INFORMATION

The reason your life isn't going well is due to one and only one factor: bad information. Bad information doesn't simply come in the form of news that is inaccurate, statistics that are made up or narratives that are designed to mislead, but in the form of beliefs, opinions, prejudices and most importantly in the form of subtle influences such as advertising, thoughts and feelings.

Underneath the physical reality that most people experience in the same manner lies a world of energies and these energies are flowing through us and around us all the time. While talk of these energies has lately become fashionable, few can perceive energy flows clearly, much less understand their sources and functions. It is these energy flows that are responsible for all that you see in the world. The narratives that people have come up with to explain how the world works are based on a very shallow view of life and are usually wrong. Let me give you a simple example of what actually happens versus what the world says happens in the same situation.

A woman walks on a street in a big city, dressed like an attorney, which is to say, dressed well and quite formally. She is talking on her phone and gets distracted by the conversation. She takes a wrong turn and ends up at a construction site, where a bunch of boys are busy working. As soon as the woman shows up, much of the work stops, the boys stare at the woman and some of them start to howl and cheer. The woman, initially horrified and then embarrassed and irritated, quickly turns around and goes back to her original route.

Typically, the world would say this woman was harassed by the boys, heckled and catcalled, etc. So what if the woman took a wrong turn? The boys didn't need to react in the manner they did. Others may say that's just how boys are and there's nothing you can do about them. Still others will allude to the woman's dress, her makeup, her style of walking or some other easily visible factor and point a finger at it.

While I agree that the behavior of boys in situations like this is often quite gross and embarrassing, there is much more going on here than you know. The boys aren't simply howling and cheering at the woman. Most of the time, boys that aren't enlightened see every woman as their mother, and they have absolutely no control over themselves as to how they respond. Energetically, their initial reaction is to assume that their mother has come to share some of her sweetness with them and they respond by literally throwing their energy into her body, because throwing energy into others' bodies is about the only thing boys know how to do.

It isn't that the boys are interested in her specifically, at least as far as their energies are concerned. Generally, boys tend to throw their energy around and just about anything in the vicinity becomes a recipient. A woman with control over her energies would easily reject the energy they are throwing at her, but most women simply don't have that ability, because they've never been taught how to develop the abilities needed to manage energy in the world. This woman has no choice but to accept the energy being thrown into her body.

Do not think that the boys on the site that are "well behaved" on the surface are any different. Even the boys on the site that are silent are doing the same thing as the boys that are vocal and animated, although just because they are silent on the outside, the world would typically not fault them in any way. The way the woman is dressed or made up has zero impact on the situation—it makes absolutely no difference whatsoever. And on top of everything else, existentially speaking, the woman is 100% at fault for wandering into a situation like this.

Most women wouldn't consider an incident like this to be a big deal overall. Some might even recount it with delight and laugh at it. While there's nothing wrong with laughing at the past, this woman has no idea what has happened energetically. The message that most often is taken away from such a situation, is that it's ok for a woman to be given something against her will, as long as nothing happened "physically." The truth is that energetically speaking, this woman hasn't just been harassed. She's been raped and she will have to carry the energy and the bad information in that energy for a long time before she realizes the impact it's had on her, if ever.

Variations of this type of behavior are seen worldwide and, in many countries, often expected, even considered "normal." There isn't anything normal about human beings getting lost, finding themselves in strange places and then getting something thrown into their bodies without them asking for it, but this is exactly what happens every day, across the world, to billions of people. This happens to you when you turn on your TV and are barraged by an advertisement, when you go to work and are asked why you are late, when you go to an airport and given "instructions" to take off your shoes, when you are pulled over by a cop and asked for your documenta-tion, and by your friends pretty much every time they speak to you or even look at you. None of these people are necessarily throwing bad energy at you on purpose, but none of them are totally unaware of it either.

THE ENERGETIC WEATHER OF THE WORLD

At this point in our Earth's history, most people on this Earth harbor some level of negativity inside them because they received it from someone else and never let it go. As I shared with you in Volume I, the experience of neg-ativity is simply your body trying to get rid of bad information in the energy that was received, which means that almost all human beings on this planet are carrying bad information within their bodies and not getting rid of it fast enough. But where does all this bad information come from?

It all starts with the fundamental misunderstandings that I shared with you in Volume I. Pain causes people to look for a way out of pain, which usually causes them to find a way to suppress it. Human beings can both avoid and suppress pain in a variety of ways, and they will usually use one thing or another to do it, just so they can carry on with their lives unimpeded. When the pain in the body accumulates, the foundation of the human being, i.e., the energy layer, becomes imbalanced. When this happens, the physical layer compensates for it and also becomes imbalanced. Once these two layers are out of balance, life starts to not feel very good. If this state continues, the psyche emerges, sometimes called "the ego." A creation of the physical body, the psyche isn't supposed to exist, but it comes "alive," starts talking and begins to cook up all kinds of ideas as to why things are not going well. These ideas tend to be based on observation of the world around the body, contain zero understanding of the underlying sickness and therefore, are completely wrong.

The body isn't just a static entity disconnected from all around it, but also a transmitter and receiver. As soon as it gets out of balance, it starts to broadcast the wrong sort of vibration. The vibration it starts to communicate, instead of being pure and simple (like the vibration given off by a tree), is now tainted with all this bad information that the psyche has cooked up. In other words, the body begins to broadcast a bunch of lies and misunderstandings of the way it believes life is going. It does this even if the human being isn't speaking, writing or communicating in "physical" ways. In other words, the very *existence* of this body now becomes disharmonious. Like an instrument that has gone out of tune because of a defect or imbalance, the body now starts to sound wrong.

When other human beings receive these vibrations, they absorb them but don't know how to filter out all the bad information and retain only the pure energy underlying them. Pretty soon, the bad information in the received energies makes its way all the way down to the foundations of the receiver, unbalancing the receiver's energy layer. Now, the receiver also starts to broadcast a bunch of bad information, and this time, they come up with new lies and misunderstandings as to why life is going poorly. It's as if one of the musicians in the orchestra starts playing out of tune, causing others in the orchestra to go out of tune as well.

When this goes on for thousands of years, you end up with a civilization where nearly everyone is broadcasting bad information almost non-stop. Pretty soon, widespread negativity takes hold. For example, most human beings nowadays tend to believe that everyone is a liar, a cheat, a criminal or in some way out to take advantage of everyone else if they can. In other words, instead of beautiful music, the world sounds like a cacophony of bad sounds.

This is the energetic weather of the world now. It is full of bad information not just on TV, the radio and social media but also on the streets, in schools and offices, in grocery stores and in most people's homes.

If you haven't ever been to the desert all by yourself (that means no phone either), especially early in the morning, just try it one day and you'll see what a dramatic difference it makes. You'll understand just how disgusting the energy weather of the world is. Some of you will not even want to come back to civilization.

This situation is compounded when many people come together and decide to live in close quarters, such as what happens in big cities. All across America, the bigger the city, the filthier it is at the energy level and the sicker and more out of balance the people who live there are.

INVISIBLE INFLUENCES

The unfortunate reality of most human beings is that they broadcast negativity even when they are polite and honest on the surface, because their energy layers are out of balance. It is impossible for people to fix this situation by simply changing their attitudes, going to therapy, taking wellness classes, using pharmaceuticals, meditating, taking yoga classes or going to a religious institution on a regular basis. As a result, you will find that no matter what you do, simply coming into contact with people who are not yogis will fill you with negativity at a layer that you aren't aware of and aren't paying attention to.

Why won't yogis give you negative energy, i.e., energy tainted with bad information? Simply because first, yogis like me tend to live alone as much as possible and second, we rarely appear in front of other people when we are not at our best. We take all the time we need to get back in tune as soon as we're out of it and only then do we start sharing anything at all. Once your intelligence starts to rise, you too, will start to become this way and prefer solitude to being among crowds all the time.

By the way, there is no such thing as "good information." Either you receive pure energy, or you receive tainted energy.

It is possible to receive bad information indirectly as well. Various substances and materials hold on to energy to varying levels, and receiving objects from other people will often give you a boatload more bad information than you would receive simply by saying hello. For example, receiving food and water from people that have a lot of issues will cause you to get sick very quickly. Unless you are sensitive enough to know what is being shared with you, you are not going to know all the ways in which you have been negatively influenced during a normal day.

UNPROCESSED INFORMATION

Another source of bad information in your system is experiences you've had in the past but have not fully integrated. In the example I gave earlier of the woman who finds herself at a construction site, it is more likely than not that the woman will simply either dismiss or "forget" that experience and move on with her life like nothing happened. Many people are being regularly taught nowadays to not care about the little things that happen to them, to "ignore" the negativity, and focus on something else. But this is exactly the wrong thing to do.

Your life does not have any "insignificant" experiences. Nothing happens in your life randomly, and nothing is meaningless from your standpoint. Every single experience you have—even the momentary appearance of a butterfly—is very significant, significant enough that your body will record it and store it for you to process later. By the time most human beings are in their teenage years, the number of experiences that have come and gone but not been processed is already too large for them to get through within a few years, at which point they hit "adulthood" and everything suddenly becomes a lot more intense.

Once you reach this point, your body becomes incapable of handling new information even at slow speeds and starts to miss things. You start to go blank or "space out" momentarily, get distracted or often get totally overwhelmed. Eventually, you go totally out of control and find yourself at the mercy of the world around you. It is at this point that the world begins to own your life experience and starts to control you in ways you don't even realize is happening. Almost everyone I've met on the streets is living a life that the world has told them to live, and they will continue to do so until the day they die without ever realizing it.

But why does your body not simply go through life and forget about the past? Why does it need to process anything at all?

Think about it this way. When you are young, everything is new. As your body goes through experiences, it needs to integrate the energy, information and intelligence it receives so that it can grow. In other words, your whole body isn't just built up of the food and drink you consume, but experiences as well. Every moment brings with it new energy, information and intelligence that your body needs to integrate in the right place. It needs to build a good foundation on which the physical body can exist. This foundation needs to be as pure as possible so that the physical body built on it has the best chance of succeeding in life.

However, the pace at which you were exposed to new experiences as a child far exceeded your capacity to make sense of it. In addition, most of the energy you were given, not just in the form of food and drink, but also in the form of parenting, TV, games and the presence of other people, was all tainted. As a child, you didn't have the intelligence to sort through all the garbage and retain only the best of what was given to you. The people around you, including your parents, probably lived equally clueless lives and didn't know how to ensure a good environment for you. Therefore, you grew up out of balance and by the time you were a teenager, you were chock full of unprocessed experiences, which mostly means you were full of unprocessed information that needed to be eliminated from your system. It's as if you spent more than a decade constantly eating, and never properly going to the toilet.

There is no way you can be a healthy teenager at this point, and it shows in the behavior of most teenagers who are out of control. At this point, society expects teenagers to be out of control. Far from recognizing what is a truly sick human being that needs help, society has concocted narratives justifying this situation, by claiming that teenagers' hormones make it impossible for them to be in control. This is utter nonsense. There is no need for teenagers to be out of control at all. The way our young people behave has everything to do with their inability to process all the bad information that has been thrown at them in the past, as well as what they receive on a near moment-to-moment basis from media of all kinds.

When this happens, you become incapable of experiencing your life fully, Time starts to slow down and eventually comes to a stop, at which point, you end up in a cycle, living the same life experiences over and over. Usually, this is when life becomes totally boring. Experimentation, risky behaviors, perversions, self-harm, addiction and suicide quickly follow.

THE ONLY SOLUTION IS SILENCE

There is absolutely no way for your body to process all that it has experienced unless you give it Time. Far from being given lectures, therapies or drugs to "fix" your behavior, what you need is Time to process all that has happened and all that is happening. When you decide to simply give your body Time to process, it slowly begins to go back to all the places it has stored past experiences and relive them, sometimes many times over. It begins to separate energy, intelligence and information and starts to throw away the information that it doesn't need. As this happens, you will find that over time, the "hurt" or "bite" associated with past experiences disappears even while the memory of those experiences continues to linger if necessary. Strange emotions (in the case of women) and feelings appear, linger and dissipate over time. All kinds of weird ideas and notions of how the world works come up and are revealed as total fabrications.

More importantly, your body starts to build a native understanding of what kind of energy is harmful and starts to change the way it makes itself available to the world. It begins to strengthen the filtering mechanism by which it keeps out what it doesn't want coming into the body in the first place. It starts to become more efficient at eliminating all the garbage that was in the body. You learn the importance of going to the toilet on a regular basis, even physically!

Unfortunately, when the foundation is fixed, the initial result in the physical body is some sort of "ugliness," such as skin issues, weight gain, loss of flexibility or strength, some sort of illness or disease. This is the way the human being works. Whatever is inside in the deeper layers is kicked out into the shallower layers, which means that once you start to heal on the inside, your physical body will no longer look as pretty as it would have if you had suppressed all the trash. If you allow this process to finish, your physical body will start to heal, but it would still take a while, as your physical body heals the slowest. It literally moves like the Earth—at a glacial pace.

And all this happens *if* you make sure to regularly spend time in silence, while also ensuring that you do not take on undue amounts of negativity in the future. This is why the path of light is difficult unless you are truly committed. It is a permanent shift in the way you want to live your life, not some temporary fix for a problem you may have noticed. While the world around you continues to get drunk to suppress the pain, takes drugs to escape the past, applies makeup to cover up flaws and creates false narratives as to what really matters, you will go in the opposite direction and you will find almost no one interested in going along with you--not even your parents, siblings or friends.

You may think that the isolation that comes with walking the path of light is a bad thing, but it is *precisely* what your body wants so it may heal, process and become normal as quickly as possible. It wants to avoid all human contact as far as possible, live in isolation, in silence, and absorb as little of the bad information being broadcast worldwide. And the more time you spend in seclusion and silence, the less you will believe in the lies being propagated, and the clearer your vision will become. Your intelligence, and your ability to literally manifest what you really need in your own life, will grow by leaps and bounds—far faster than you believe is possible. And only when you are totally done with the process will you be ready to even care about anyone else.

Don't get me wrong—this path does not preclude you from going to school or to college, getting a job, having a relationship and so on. But the *way* you go about doing everything will be radically different than all your peers, which is why a very small number of people even think about this path until they are older and realize that they wasted their time in youth when they had the most energy and the best chance of finishing quickly.

So, assuming that you do, in fact, want to go down this path still, how do you practice?

THE PRACTICE

Every day, sit in silence, with your eyes open, for up to 20 minutes. That's all.

What does "silence" mean? It means that you do absolutely nothing else but sit silently: no eating or drinking, no conversations, no phone, no music or TV, no alarms, no pets, no sleeping, no walking around, no looking out the window, no closing your eyes. Basically, all you are doing at that point, is sitting alone and breathing for 20 minutes, *with your eyes open*. Do not do this practice on a bus, in the mall, or at a party. You don't have to focus anywhere in particular because this isn't meditation. You don't have to do anything about your thoughts, feelings, memories or any bodily movements (e.g., twitches) you might experience. You can wear anything you like as long as it's comfortable.

Understand that 20 minutes isn't a rule, but a measure of your Time. Different people will experience 20 minutes very differently. If you get distracted, just come back and continue the practice. If you are lost in thought for longer than 20 minutes, don't worry about it. Do not set an alarm to tell you when 20 minutes is up. Rely on your natural sense. Most importantly, never force yourself to continue when you don't want to. In the beginning, most of you will struggle to stay silent even for a minute or two without having something to look at or focus on. It's alright. Just keep practicing day after day and you will soon understand what it is that you are experiencing. At some point, your own understanding will evolve the practice and you must go with it instead of sticking to a rigid rule.

The time of the day when you do this is not at all important. You are welcome to do this anytime, or at a different time every day. With practice, your body will learn to take full advantage of this practice and will start to work on processing all that needs processing at an accelerated pace as soon as you become silent.

EXCEPTIONS FOR WOMEN

You are allowed (and encouraged) to sit silently with other women who are also doing this practice, as long as you do not interact with each other in *any* way, not even by looking at each other.

EXCEPTIONS FOR TROUBLED INDIVIDUALS

If you are an individual that is at risk of committing suicide, self-harm or harm to others, do not do this practice in isolation. Make sure there is someone in your home (in another room, for example) who can get to you if necessary. They should not be sitting around watching you, but they should be there for you if necessary. If you are indeed extremely troubled or simply cannot be alone, this practice is not for you.

RESULTS OF PRACTICE

If you do this practice diligently, within 6 months your life will undergo a dramatic change. This will happen because allowing your body to process what's happened will radically speed up the Time in your life. As your body learns to process inputs faster, it will welcome new experiences at a faster rate and your life will start to become a blur. Do not worry if this happens, because the "blur" is a situation where your body hasn't fully learned to focus on what it really cares about. As it understands what it cares about, your attention will be subconsciously directed only towards things, people and experiences you care about, while the rest will be "on auto," so to speak. This is called clarity, and it will arrive after a very long time.

AN INVITATION

Regardless of gender, if you are interested in seriously walking the path of light, you are welcome to move to Tucson, along with whoever and whatever you care about. Do not underestimate the influence that many spiritually inclined young people can have on a town. You do not need to live with me, or even close to me. Simply being in the presence of others who are also interested in working on themselves will make a big difference in your spiritual life. I can tell you from experience that Tucson has the perfect weather for spiritual work, year-round. You are welcome to establish little cohorts in whatever city or town you live as well, but do not make it a commercial enterprise or a club, as the practices, at the end of the day, are there to encourage you to become a fully-fledged individual, not a member of some religious or spiritual society. This means it is best that any such effort be publicized entirely by word of mouth, instead of organized modes such as social media.

The next few chapters will focus on various aspects of practical living and how you can give yourself the best chance of moving forward.

ATTITUDE

THESE INSTRUCTIONS ARE FOR GOD

You may be wondering why any of the guidelines I am about to lay out would be implemented by you. After all, if you, as the spirit, have already laid out a plan for your life and are here to live it, why would anything I say have an effect? If you aren't in charge of the life you're living, nor do you have the power to *do*, but only the power to enable things to happen, how can the instructions of any guru or yogi ever have any impact? In other words, why would you change your life at all?

Here's the truth of what I am saying in this book: they aren't always oriented towards you, the spirit, the body you are in or even your psyche. Most of what I am going to say in this volume is targeted at that deeper intelligence that has the power to do things, aka God. I am going to speak to the God in your being because it is God that needs instructions from a higher level of intelligence to make changes in a specific manner.

The thing about God is that God doesn't know you, nor does God know the world. It's as if there is someone running a machine in perfect order, but the one running the machine neither knows nor cares what the machine accomplishes in the world, nor does it care about all the stories others are telling about the machine. God knows what the weather around the machine looks like and can handle whenever the weather changes in order to keep the machine in tip top condition, but God doesn't care if the machine doesn't actually perform what is "expected" of it on any given day.

People who surrender to God (or are *surrendered* to God), find that their lives fall apart in violent, unpredictable and disastrous ways as God simply ignores your world and does whatever is correct. Unless you lived with me, you would not survive such turmoil. So what God needs are instructions that are going to change your life in a very specific manner that will not cause too much chaos. These instructions need to fit the world in which we live *now*, not the world that Jesus lived in, for example. This is why I am telling you to never read any spiritual treatise, religious book, self-help manual or other such nonsense once you've committed to the path I've laid out, because all that will do is confuse your life. This is also why yogis and gurus keep coming down and sharing new instructions as time passes, while keeping the fundamentals the same so that you, the people who want to live a beautiful life, can succeed. Truth never changes, but wisdom needs updating as time passes.

It is also for this reason that this volume has an expiration date: the year 2144. When the world changes, you must no longer follow these guidelines, but the guidance of whoever is on Earth at that point and interested in speaking to humanity as a whole.

WHY GOD WON'T LISTEN TO YOU

If God listens to instructions, can *you* give God instructions and thereby make changes in your life as you see fit? Sure, but only if you have a higher level of intelligence operating in your life. Even though you are the spirit, you are working with such a low level of intelligence at the moment that God will not listen to you. God will not even listen to the ultimate power in the universe. God only listens to one specific manifestation of intelligence: the feminine kind. In fact, God only listens to the highest level of feminine intelligence.

The manifestation of the ultimate power in the universe is feminine in nature. She wishes that I refer to Her as the Divine Feminine. Other yogis and monks have variously called her the Divine Mother and such, but in my life, She has come to me as a partner. No, I am not saying that there is an actual human being in my life that acts as the Divine Feminine. The Divine Feminine is a level of intelligence that has become a part of my being. She knows all about creation and how it is put together. It is Her that gives instructions that God carries out in the life of human beings on this Earth. And it is She who is writing this book, while the human being that I am is only an instrument.

God will listen to Her. God will not listen to you, which is another good reason you shouldn't pray to God or ask for things from God, because you'd simply be wasting your energy.

DON'T ASK FOR STUFF

There are people all over the world who will claim—correctly—that when they asked for things, they received them. If God isn't listening, how is this possible? This is possible because you don't have to specifically ask God for things. Simply asking for things will make them happen in your life. Perhaps you've heard the phrase "Ask and ye shall receive"? It is a law in our existence. Whatever you ask for, you will receive—not instantly, but at some point.

If this is true, why don't people simply ask for whatever they want, receive it and be happy? Well, people *are*, in fact, asking for all sorts of things, mostly without even realizing it and they *are*, in fact, being made to receive them. The problem isn't the law or that it is functioning incorrectly. The problem is simply this: you, the spirit, have already laid out a life you want to live, and it contains everything you want. Yes, you came here to experience all that you truly desire, not the false desires that the world has convinced you that you need or want. But when you ask for something, your life will literally change track—derail, in other words—and start moving in a direction that first, prepares you to receive what you asked for and second be given what you asked for. When this happens, all that you truly wanted will get delayed while your whole life is re-routed to receive what you asked for.

Unfortunately, when most people ask for something, they don't understand what *else* is going to come with what they asked for, and most of the time, they don't want all that other stuff. For example, when people ask for a yacht, they don't realize just how burdensome the whole experience is going to be, just how much sacrifice is going to be needed to maintain the damn thing, not to mention the number of idiots they're going to have to deal with to keep that yacht in working order. Meanwhile, the rest of their life might change too, exposing them to people, places and situations they just don't enjoy. This kind of thing has happened to a great many people around the world. However, considering how good the world is at convincing people that they've done the right thing when they've done exactly the opposite, most people never recover and get back to their original life. They continue to believe that they're doing well.

What you need to remember is that everything you really need will come to you when you really need it, but only if you don't ask for things you don't need. This includes money, courage, strength, whatever. You don't have to ask. So, whenever you feel like you need to ask for things, just shut up. Stop making wishes, even frivolously.

STOP TRYING TO HELP

It's important that you stop caring about the world. You don't have to disconnect your phone, turn off social media or live off the grid. You don't have to stop watching the news or discussing politics with your friends. These kinds of things will happen to you when the time is right, so you don't have to force them. What you do need to do is *stop trying to help*, no matter what the situation. Let me give you a simple example.

If you live in any big city in America, you will find groups of people that are referred to as the homeless. These people tend to live in difficult situations, have little comfort, no peace and are often surrounded by criminality, violence, drug use and many other societal ills. In cities like Los Angeles, homelessness is so widespread that at least in certain parts of town, you will find the homeless on every inch of the sidewalk. Your first instinct may be to help these people in some way, to give them change, perhaps buy them food and so on. Or perhaps, driven by your feelings, you decide to get serious and plunge yourself into solving the homelessness crisis. Unfortunately, everything you do in order to help the homeless will only make the problem worse.

Do not think that the homeless are there "by accident." Life does not randomly kick people into situations like that. The homeless are in dire need of one thing and only one thing: Time. Destitution is life's way of stripping human beings of all else, forcing them to pay attention to their own life and giving them Time to work out issues in their lives. We, as a civilization, can support the homeless by providing the bare minimum of shelter and food so that they do not have to spend energy on those things and can therefore, give themselves the Time they need to figure things out. However, if a human being is unwilling to use whatever they already have been given to move forward in life, everything given to them will go to waste. There are unfortunately so many homeless people that are now beyond the point where they can help themselves (e.g., mentally ill, severely addicted, disabled and so on) that you, as a young person, *cannot* and *should not* waste your life trying to move them forward, because, to truly help them, you would essentially have to carry them all the way to their destination.

So, what do you do when you come across a homeless person? Nothing. What do you do when someone asks you to participate in an activity to help the homeless? Nothing. What do you do when someone wants you to vote on a resolution to help the homeless? Nothing. Don't think that this works only when you aren't being affected. You must do this even if you are being affected. For example, what do you do when the city raises taxes to help the homeless? Nothing. What if a homeless encampment is built right next to your home? Do nothing. Even if the world does something that specifically disadvantages you to help the homeless, do nothing.

In other words, you simply ignore the homelessness situation, totally. You allow it to go wherever it does, grow, shrink or fall apart. You simply refuse to participate, engage, help or hinder in any way. Do not willfully go and throw your trash wherever the homeless are, call them names, lecture them, etc. Just forget about them completely.

BECOME TOTALLY IRRESPONSIBLE

What you do for the homeless, i.e., nothing, is exactly what you should do *for every single worldly concern.* The people in your life may not like the way this sounds, but you must become utterly and totally irresponsible for the world and all its problems. Don't bother with saving the whales, conserving the environment, voting for the right political party or even saying hello to your neighbors. It doesn't matter if these things happen or don't happen in your life. It doesn't matter if thoughts about your involvement in the world come up or don't come up when you spend time in silence. Understand that beneath all the narratives of the world lies the true reality where your body wants to live. If you are focused on the way that the world wants you to see things, you will not arrive at the reality of the situation. You will not see what you really need to do to make the world a better place.

In other words, you must totally disengage from all that you really don't care about, no matter how much the world wants you to care.

Do not misunderstand what I am saying. There are people all around the world that willfully go about destroying things, robbing stores, raping women, terrorizing people or even throwing their garbage on the streets and acting like hoodlums. They justify this type of behavior by blaming the system for all their woes and claim to be bringing it down this way. People like that are only strengthening the worst parts of our civilization because adding energy to a system only makes it stronger, not weaker. All the terrorists have ever done, for example, is make the world much more prison-like and less free. You must never follow these sorts of examples.

Whenever you engage in destructive behavior, your life will take a turn for the worse. This is true whether you kill an animal, uproot a tree, mow the lawn, harass a woman, criticize someone specifically, spread your garbage or simply lie, cheat and steal. It's irrelevant to me as to what happens to the world when you do such things, but *you* certainly will fall into darkness and most likely not recover. So, what should your attitude be?

NON-VIOLENT NON-COMPLIANCE

Non-violent non-compliance simply means that you *do what you must,* and you *do not do what you shouldn't.* In the beginning, you will find that putting "do what you must" into practice is difficult, because only a higher level of intelligence will have the clarity to decide whether you must do something. But you will certainly not be unclear about the fact that you are unclear! And when you are in doubt, *don't.* Let me give you some examples.

You are hanging out with your friends, one of them decides that they want to watch a pornographic movie and you are unsure that you want to participate. Just leave. Don't sit around convincing others not to watch the movie or trying to get them to see the light. You found yourself in bad company. Get out of there and stay away from people with poor taste.

You are waiting at a bus stop and a homeless man comes around asking for change. You feel guilty, but you aren't sure you'll be helping by giving them money. Ignore them or just walk away. Don't wait for the situation to "resolve itself."

You are in a meeting and your boss demands that you commit to delivering a result within a certain time frame. If you don't want to do it, ignore them, leave or just say no. Don't argue and don't try to convince them as to why it's a bad idea. If they refuse to listen, forget about them—you aren't on the hook for making other people successful or happy and you certainly didn't come here to be a slave. Understand this clearly—this has nothing to do with whether something *can* be done, and everything with whether *you care about doing it.* Yes, this sort of behavior may get you fired or disciplined, but if you're walking the path of light, this is the way. The path of light is fraught with great risk at every turn.

By the way, if you have a boss, parent, coach, etc. that has even a little bit of intelligence, they will make a request of you and ask you for your opinion. They will not make demands.

Here's another one: your elderly female neighbor knocks on your door and asks you for help because a strange man was at her door a few minutes ago, trying to get in and she is afraid for her life. At best, tell her to call the police and close the door. I mean it. Do not *ever* get involved in anyone else's life unless they are your life partner, or your children. By the way, all children are your children—it's ok to get involved if you see them in danger *and there are no other adults already involved.*

Finally, here's a difficult one. You are walking on the street and see a man throwing up and in bad shape. As you pass by, he starts begging you for help because he's had too much fentanyl and he's going to die if he doesn't get treatment. In the US, there are emergency services available via 911. Call 911, get them the details of the situation (not your details) *and leave.* Don't wait around for the person to die in your presence and certainly don't sit around trying to help and comfort them. You have absolutely no idea just how poisonous such a situation is, energetically speaking.

The truth about life on this Earth is that wisdom has always been in serious short supply, while idiotic stories championing saviorship, rescue and other such worthless concepts are everywhere. People with little understanding of true spirituality have misinterpreted the words of Jesus, the Buddha and other saints and sages to mean that they are widely applicable in every situation. They are not, *especially* in the case of women. Women should *never* stick around to help strangers—ever.

If you are a first responder, a nurse, a doctor or other such professional, I am sorry for you, because your life is nothing but a series of situations where you are consuming other people's poison, aka extremely high amounts of energy combined with bad information on a near-constant basis.

Remember this: the world is not important. Civilization is not important. Other people are not important. Life is important, and at the moment, the only life you know is yours. Focus on it to the exclusion of all else. Only when you start to grow intelligent, see life clearly and become inclusive can you really embrace others and do the right thing for them. This happens only when you're enlightened. Until then, forget about the world and its problems.

LIMIT HUMAN CONTACT

Understand something very clearly—your life is entirely the result of the way you have lived so far. Now that you are interested in following the way of truth, beauty and love, you must hold everyone else to the same standard. Do not expect help, but do not refuse it either if it is given to you freely, and without you asking for it. For example, when I had a motorcycle accident in LA, I didn't ask for help. Some people who saw me crash flagged down another driver, who then hailed a cop, who then called a tow truck. It was the tow truck driver that dropped me off at an emergency room—I didn't make a single request, nor did I reject the help offered. I was happy to accept my fate, whatever the hell it was. This is how you must be. Be willing to accept your fate.

However, do not help anyone else, because the *only* way to help anyone on this Earth is to shoulder at least part of their burden. Specifically, this means you will be taking on some of the bad information they have failed to work out in their own lives, and you will be working it out on their behalf, but in your own life.

The principle behind all this advice is very simple: if you want to walk the path of light and finish, you must conserve as much of your precious energy as you can and minimize the amount of bad information, negativity or bad energy you receive in the world. If you are serious about enlightening yourself, creating a beautiful life for yourself and truly helping humanity from a place of freedom, clarity and intelligence, you cannot afford to take on anyone else's burden while you are on the way. If you help other people, you will not finish. The choice is yours.

In my life, I was specifically given to many people to help them, so I did. I have, in fact, waited next to a fentanyl addict in severe distress until the ambulance arrived. I have, in fact, counseled many women on how to deal with strangers. I have, in fact, bought food for many homeless women in LA when they requested me to do so. And of course, I have consumed more poison from more people and worked it out in my own life than I can possibly recount. But this was *my life*, and I was specifically directed by a power beyond this Earth to do this. I had no choice in the matter, nor did I have any doubts as to what to do. I consumed the poison I did because I had to understand the nature of the energy in those situations and share this wisdom with you. And because of all the poison I consumed, I spent most of the last 42 years in very poor physical health.

But now that my spiritual service has ended, I tell you I throw people out of my life faster than they can say hello. I am living the truth that I am sharing with you.

If you want to progress as fast as possible, you must limit human contact to the bare minimum necessary. Don't make friends and don't be "sociable," as far as possible. Do not force yourself to do this in the beginning but understand that you will naturally get there one day. And one fine day, if you find yourself alone, don't judge yourself.

Your attitude should be simply that you want the best of what life has to offer, that you are willing to be prepared by life so that you are ready to receive it fully and that you are willing to go without it as long as necessary while you are being prepared. No substitutes are needed, nor welcome.

DISCOMFORT

The one thing that is common to all people who walk the path of darkness and is in fact a clear indicator that they do walk the path of darkness, is that they live in comfort and not just a little bit of comfort, but extremely unhealthy levels of comfort. When I speak of comfort in this chapter, I am talking specifically about physical comfort, the kind that our civilization has totally bought into. At least in the United States, the level of comfort that people are experiencing is insane. But why is comfort a bad thing?

A little bit of comfort is a very good thing, because it keeps you grounded on Earth, a concept I'll discuss later in this book. However, the opposite of comfort is what our bodies (and that means all layers) rely on to stay healthy. To help you understand this, let me give you an analogy to explain how the human mechanism is supposed to stay clean: laundry.

HOW THE BODY STAYS CLEAN

Laundry requires at least three elements to be successful: a solvent (e.g., water), a detergent (e.g., soap), and a method of agitation. The detergent helps in lifting the dirt and solvent carries it away, but without agitation, you won't get a good clean. When I was traveling in South India, I saw women on the riverbanks beating their laundry with little bats, literally beating the dirt out of those clothes. In fact, this is how gurus used to be with disciples in the past sometimes, but now we don't use such violent methods, even on clothes. Today, in most washing machines, you will find a central agitator, or a drum that spins causing the clothes to tumble. It is this principle that your body relies on to stay clean.

When you live in discomfort, you will experience all kinds of agitation. Imagine you are living many thousands of years ago in the forest. You don't have any clothing, so you are cold. The ground is either soggy, dry or full of sharp stuff like branches and rocks. As you walk, branches on the trees sometimes cut into your skin. Flies and mosquitoes endlessly harass you. You are probably hungry and tired because it's not easy to find food in the forest—you must either hunt or gather. And all this works if it's nice out. If the weather is bad, you are probably shivering, hunkering down in whatever little shelter you can find and probably at your wits end because you can't even sleep peacefully. After all, if you've found some shelter, so have other creatures that are interested in "sharing" it with you.

COLD, TIRED AND HUNGRY

Whenever you are cold, tired and hungry, you will be agitated: energetically, physically, emotionally and psychologically. When this happens, your body will kick out all the bad information it's been holding on to. This is why when people are agitated, they tend to start swearing, acting in erratic ways and generally being idiots. Once all the negativity leaves, people calm down, even if the external situation hasn't changed much. Sometimes people confuse this process to be "acceptance," but it is nothing of the sort. Your body is totally ok with discomfort—it's only when bad information is inside that it wants to get rid of the garbage as fast as possible.

Where does all that bad information go? It is taken away by the elements: sunshine, rain, the Earth and the wind. This is the mechanism by which we are expected to stay free of negativity, free of bad information, be healthy and feel good.

Now compare the way we used to live to the way you live now. When was the last time you walked barefoot in nature, got wet in bad weather, hurt yourself because you brushed against some sharp bushes, or more importantly, were cold, tired and hungry at the same time? Those last three—cold, tiresomeness and hunger—are *the* most important things you must experience at least once every day, if you want to stay healthy, rid yourself of bad information, stay positive and grow more intelligent. This is how most of my life has been--especially whenever I have worked intensely on something spiritual--and even today, it hasn't changed much. Let me share with you a bit about how I live.

I don't use my air conditioner, except for a few moments to remove a bit of excess moisture in the home on summer nights. In Summer, it is set to 90 F in the day and 85 F in the night, which means it hardly ever turns on in the desert climate that I live in. I have at least one window or door open 24 hours a day, meaning my home is more or less at the same temperature as the shade under a tree. I don't have any furniture in my house, which means I eat on the floor, sleep on the floor, relax on the floor, etc. I eat twice a day, once after I work out and once in the evening, with no snacks in between. This means that at least on the way home from the gym (which I walk to), I am extremely cold, tired and hungry. If I need to go distances, I don't drive a car, but ride a motorcycle whether it's 119 F and dry or 20 F and raining. Moreover, I wear exactly one single layer of clothing no matter the season or the weather.

Don't think I am doing this by choice. The Divine Feminine refuses to let me live in comfort because She insists that I must be 100% clean and clear of all negativity at all times. You will never see me not smiling or happy. In fact, I am usually ecstatic. In addition to all this discomfort, I regularly find myself experiencing cuts, scrapes, bruises and injuries thanks to walking barefoot in nature, wandering among cacti and so on. All this is extremely healthy.

WHAT CAN YOU ENDURE?

I am not telling you this to brag, but to help you see that you must live in *as much discomfort as you can stand.* Get rid of that couch and all that soft stuff that makes you feel like a corpse in training. Forget about air conditioning, iced drinks and other comfort-oriented measures if you can stand the weather (but don't torture the body either). Throw away all those layers of clothing that insulate you from the natural weather of the Earth, keeping only what you need to live and work. And stop using motorized transportation everywhere. You must allow yourself to be caught in a rainstorm occasionally and suffer the consequences. It's important! Additionally, make sure to spend as much time in nature as possible and deal with the harshness of the weather, the flies and mosquitoes without aids (i.e., don't use sunscreen or bug spray).

How far you go, and what you do, is up to you and the way you live today. Don't be an idiot and try to survive winter without heating if you live in Minnesota, for example, but don't make it so comfortable that your body doesn't feel the weather at all. Don't starve yourself of food and water; living in discomfort does not mean torturing the body. In fact, let your body decide what is good. I can assure you that your body will pick a far greater level of discomfort than you've assumed is necessary.

ALLOW YOUR BODY TO SENSE

I see many people in the US who never take off their sunglasses. This kind of thing confuses the body, because it relies on, among other things, vision to decide if the environment is safe. If it is too bright for you to go outside, it's too bright! If your eyes need to adjust, they will. Otherwise, it means your body doesn't want to go outside, and you must not force it. If you lived in the desert, you would know, like all the animals here do, that it is not a good idea to be out and about between 10 AM and 4 PM in summer. Don't fool the body into believing it's safer than it is, using stupid tricks and technologies like ice packs and chilled drinks. It is these kinds of tactics that are causing people to get sicker over time instead of healthier.

This kind of sense works energetically as well. You should know before you walk into a room if you are going to be accosted or harassed in some way. You should know if an environment is safe enough for you to be in without having to be assured. And you should know if the situation is about to change so you can leave before you become a victim. Your body has the capability to sense the energetic weather of the world, so allow it to develop and use that sense.

When I was in Los Angeles, I was near constantly in places where the environment was horrible, not because I chose such places, but because Los Angeles is dirty everywhere—energetically speaking. However, my senses were constantly on alert and knew what to do if things got really bad. I was once inside a department store buying weekly groceries when I sensed that a homeless man, who was also an addict, was about to walk into the store and create a mess. About a minute before the man himself even walked into the store, I pointed him out to a store clerk, told her he was about to create a problem and walked off to a different part of the same store and continued shopping. A minute later the man walked into the store, started throwing alcohol bottles off the shelves onto the ground, yelled and screamed and started making a ruckus. I myself was surprised as my body calmly went about finishing shopping, paying and leaving through a different exit without ever directly encountering the chaos on the other side of the store.

This kind of thing has been true all my life. I have always known when trouble is about to happen in any situation and usually my body simply finds another place to be and continues its business unimpeded. I have literally crossed the street ahead of time to avoid a fight between teenagers on the streets, gotten off buses before troublemakers got on, left conference rooms before people got into an argument, calmly ridden my motorcycle around groups of people just before they started a riot and so on.

Your body needs to sense the environment—both physically and energetically—to know what to do every moment. It is precisely because people are denying themselves the chance to be sensible that they are relying more and more on sources of information, like weather reports. You should know if it's about to rain. You should know if it's going to get unseasonably hot or cold. You should know if there's going to be an overnight freeze. I know this because my body does know—I never look up weather reports. My body even goes and buys the right groceries ahead of time depending on the weather so I can stay warmer or cooler as necessary. This level of intelligence needs to come into your life so you can live effortlessly and with clarity.

CLARITY EXPOSES THE SUBCONSCIOUS

You may wonder if I am clairvoyant, as in whether I can see the future before it happens. Yes, but this is not some kind of superpower. As I've described to you, all experience begins within you and is slowly manifested on the outside. This means that whatever experience you are about to have is available to your subconscious before it becomes conscious. All of you know what is about to happen, and some of you even "have a feeling" sometimes. The problem for most of you, is that your bodies are so full of bad information that your subconscious is in utter chaos all the time and consequently cannot clearly share with you what is about to happen.

If I raise your energy (or perhaps you take a drug and get there—don't try this), you'll encounter your subconscious which, if unclear, will create all kinds of weird hallucinations and bad experiences for you. This is why this type of experience is given by gurus to people only after a long period of cleansing and catharsis. As you progress along the spiritual path, which you can do by practicing all I am sharing in this book, your subconscious will begin to clear and one fine day, it will become completely silent.

Then, and only then, you will know what is about to happen before it happens with utter surety. Now, don't think this applies to stupid things like the stock market. You will not use whatever clairvoyance you have to make money or take advantage of other people. By the time you see with the clarity I do, you will be enlightened, and have zero interest in survival, money-making or manipulating the future in some way. But your body will benefit because it will use this ability to make sure it stays in good places, in clean environments and keeps its energy and intelligence level way up, all the time.

By the way, most of what you read, hear on the radio, watch on TV, or see on your phone or at the movies is entirely a product of people coming in touch with their subconscious, encountering utter chaos and concocting a garbage narrative out of it. If your bodily filter isn't functioning perfectly, consuming media in general is akin to consuming food that other people have regurgitated after failing to digest it properly, because it is literally chock full of poison that other people have thrown up. Almost all sources of media are just garbage bins for just about everyone to throw whatever they want into. This is why people on the spiritual path tend to disconnect from all such sources. In your case, I'll let you decide what you want to do.

By the way, there are points in this book where I say that I'll let you decide whether or not you should do something. I am saying that because those who read this book and start the spiritual journey in earnest will find, at some point, that they have *no choice* but to follow the practices and suggestions in this book. The Divine Feminine will guarantee that you cannot disobey, which means that you are being surrendered. So, when it comes to certain things, She has decided to give you a choice in the matter, instead of just forcing you to conform.

But what do you do if you have no choice but to work in a bad environment, at least for now? Discomfort will help you cleanse, but is there something you can do to make sure that you absorb as little of the negativity in your environment as possible? Yes, this is what the next chapter is about.

CLOTHING

Far from being simply about comfort and style, clothing is a direct consequence of human intelligence realizing that it is now in environments that
are no longer pure and safe all the time.

Your clothing is your first—and only—defense against negativity in
the world in which we all live. The problem with the body's way of dealing
with bad information is that it absorbs everything it encounters, then filters,
and finally eliminates all that it doesn't want. While extremely effective, it
is slow, and not built to handle the level of bad information that is around
us. Even if you go to your neighborhood grocery store, there are days you
may find yourself jostled around by the crowds and be practically molested
by everyone's energies. In such a situation, your body will want to leave—
which is the right thing to do—but if you don't have a choice (e.g., you
work there!), your only salvation lies in wearing the right clothing. Let me
share with you an experience I had that will help you understand.

A SCHOOLGIRL IN LA

As I did on many mornings in Los Angeles, I was walking in the cool,
dewy sunshine down 6th Street towards a coffee shop where I would often
sit down to write a blog post on the issues with the way teenage girls were
living in Los Angeles and what the consequences would be. Most of what

I learned there I'll only share with women if they ask me about it, but the experience of living in LA was a real eye opener for me as to just how bad things had gotten for our young women without them knowing what to do about it.

Now it just so happened that this coffee shop was right next to a high school, and I had to often pass by throngs of young people to get to the cafe. On this particular day, as I approached the high school, I noticed a car pull up and drop off a girl across the street from the school entrance. I knew instantly that this girl was the kind that gets herself in trouble, and as I watched, she darted across the street, holding onto whatever she had—a bag, some other accessories and such—trying to get to the entrance quickly.

In addition to many other senses I've developed, one of them is knowing exactly who is paying attention to who and how, without ever looking at them directly. I can sense, for example, when someone is paying attention to a woman in a disgusting manner (i.e., lustfully instead of lovingly) even if the two people are quite far away from me. I call this 'sensing poison' and I've had this sense all my life. In the case of this high school girl, as soon as she got out of the car, I instantly sensed a strong current of poison being directed toward her and I followed the current all the way down the street to a young man staring very lustfully at this girl.

This girl wasn't dressed in a revealing manner. In fact, she was dressed almost perfectly for the situation—fully covered up. The poisonous attention she was receiving had absolutely nothing to do with her dress, and everything to do with her *way*, which is an energetic thing. She was basically throwing her energy around and inviting just about everyone and everything to take what they wanted from her. But the fact that she was, in fact, mostly covered up is what helped her deflect most of that poisonous attention instead of absorbing it. This is what good clothing can do for you—protect you when you don't even know you're being attacked.

THE RIGHT CLOTHING

The right clothing is always loose, light or bright colored, only one layer thick and covering as much of your body as you are comfortable with wearing. It is never tight or body-hugging, never dark or black, and never exposing parts of your body to the surrounding environment—with exceptions. You need clothing to be loose and have exactly one layer because it helps the body sense the environment as well as breathe properly. Everything else has to do with energy.

Just like light colors reflect visible light, they reflect all energy directed towards them. Wearing light (ideally white) ensures that *only* your energy is available to you, and not the garbage that everyone else is throwing out or throwing specifically in your direction.

It doesn't matter who you are and how you are dressed—understand that people's attention isn't necessarily directed towards you because you don't have enough clothing on. It is in fact your energy that causes people to look at you or to turn away from you. If you are already the sort of human being (typically feminine) that attracts attention, then having little clothing to cover your body will only cause you to absorb whatever kind of energy is being directed at you. While people like me rarely look at anyone else, most of the attention you will receive in public will be negative, i.e., tainted with bad information, and therefore will make your body work harder to stay clean and clear.

Women attract attention not because they are sexy, pretty or whatever, but because they tend to have energy that is inherently sweet and bodies that are naturally made to receive. As a woman, there's little you can do about this. In fact, those qualities are good for you—you just need to learn to make the most of them without becoming a victim of circumstance.

CLOTHING FOR MEN

This section applies to individuals with an exceptional level of masculinity, i.e., those with far greater masculinity than femininity. Your exposure to the world is not fraught with as much danger as it is for women, so you can be a bit lax. Additionally, most of the work that your body is expected to do is physical, which means that if you are the kind of male that is active physically, clothing becomes less and less important. In this sense, it is true that the harder you work with your body—especially in sunshine—the less clothing you need in those situations to protect yourself from the energy of other people. As your body exerts itself, a great many things are taken care of.

Regardless it is a good idea for you to wear clothing that covers, at the very minimum, your heart (the area in the center of your chest, not your physical heart) and your genitals (for society's sake!). Yes, even today, it is unnecessary from an energy standpoint for a man to cover anything but his heart. I have seen many males who walk around with their shirts unbuttoned so that their hearts are visible, which is exactly the wrong thing to do. As a male, a lot of your energy is given away through the heart and you must not leave it unprotected.

When you proceed on the spiritual path, you will find that initially your body gets weaker. As it does, it will want to put on clothing that covers more and more of the body—and you should go along with it. Do not fight your body's clothing preferences.

CLOTHING FOR WOMEN

Women are in serious trouble with clothing nowadays. Everywhere it seems some new kind of trend arrives that encourages women to expose themselves even more than before. A lot of this is being pushed onto women under the guise of freedom, but it is little more than society's hunger for sweetness manifesting as the exploitation of women.

If you go into nature, especially into an area with lots of trees and flowers, the one thing you will notice is that the place is *sweet*. This is essentially a trait of the feminine (not women specifically), but since women embody exceptional levels of femininity, their presence generally tends to be sweet. Our civilization, however, is hyper-masculine in nature, and consequently, people in general have lost touch with their femininity and become bitter in a very real, energetic sense. This, more than anything else, is causing so much hunger among so many for sugar and sweetness in general, in every form.

The rise of pornography, child molestation and the disgusting portrayal of women in many forms of media are all simply stupid ways that humanity has found by which it can satisfy its craving for sweetness. Younger and younger women are being pressed into service and literally being squeezed of their energy to feed a hungry populace that has no sweetness in their own lives.

Combined with the feminine trait that makes it prone to receive more than give, women are suffering on two fronts simultaneously: they are being depleted of their energies, and they are being filled with the poison that comes with negative attention from others seeking their sweetness.

As a woman, if you want to stay healthy, safe and clear, you *must* cover yourself up as much as you can endure. There are cultures where this is being forced upon women, which is a bad idea—the feminine must never be forced, in any way! Those cultures will pay for their stupidity—there's nothing you can do about it—but as a young woman in a society that allows you some freedom, understand that if you don't cover yourself up, you will pay the price and so will the world in which you live.

As is true for men, parts of your body that are worked hard do not generally need to be covered up. This, for most women nowadays, means the hands and face. However, there is much more tendency among women to *internalize* the energy they receive, which means unless women are working hard *emotionally* as well, they will not be clean and clear. It is for this reason that women are encouraged to seek a stable relationship and work hard at the emotional side of things, even teaching men to love, because it exercises the internals of a woman and keeps her clean and clear.

For now, at the very minimum, seek to cover every part of your body except your face and hands (yes, even your neck and feet must be covered fully) with a single layer of light-colored, loose-fitting clothing (this includes shoes). This will ensure that you are protected in every situation against negative attention.

It is no longer important for women to cover their heads. Head coverings are meaningful only in cases where women have progressed spiritually to the point where they have realized that they want love to come into their lives. If they are at this point, they may signify to the ultimate power in the universe that they are ready to invite love into their lives by covering their heads. If you are a woman in this state, you're welcome to cover your head with a hoodie, a helmet, a scarf, a tiara, sunglasses, a hat—whatever—existence doesn't care about such things. If you are clear that you want to invite love into your life, you are welcome to embellish or cover the top of your head to signify that fact.

CLOTHING FOR CHILDREN

When I say "children," I am only referring to those who haven't reached puberty. It is totally unnecessary for children to wear any clothing whatsoever. They are in no danger, energetically speaking, from being poisoned excessively or depleted of their sweetness. Yes, they too have sweetness others want but at that age they replenish themselves easily. However, you know very well how some people in the world look at children. So, if you want them to be safe, dress your children in the same way that I've suggested the women be dressed. Otherwise, let the children wear whatever they want—or not!

CLOTHING AT HOME

If you are at home, or perhaps you are wealthy enough to have your own private island where there are no prying eyes, you shouldn't wear anything—man, woman or child. Especially in front of children, it is important that parents be naked as far as possible and allow children to see that there isn't anything wrong with the body as is, no matter how fat or thin or misshapen it may be.

Your body absolutely *loves* to be naked outside, as some of you have no doubt experienced. It is good for it to be exposed to sunshine, wind, rain, the Earth, the sky and all the sweetness and harshness of this beautiful planet. Occasionally, you must give yourself (and everyone you care about enough to be ok with being naked in front of) a chance to go experience nature totally naked. Even today, there are many places in our woods where this is possible. Please do not do this in so-called "nudist" enclaves. The point of this exercise is for you to experience pure energy, not be naked in front of random strangers. Obviously, it's best if you do this alone.

So far, we've talked about what you can do to ensure that you limit exposure to negativity and protect yourself in cases where you cannot. Now we'll go into detail about consuming energy directly, in the form of food and water.

WATER

Water, of all the elements, has the greatest impact on your well-being. Your relationship with water is a gauge as to how good you feel. People that are always happy—like me—have a very sweet, intimate, loving, beautiful, kind and in every way fantastic relationship with water. You'll notice this with children as well, who are drawn to water like bees (or bears!) to nectar. The way you treat water will have an immediate and massive impact on your well-being starting on day one.

HOW TO STORE WATER

Water must never be stored in an open or transparent container. The thing about water is that it has intelligence, memory and little information. It is flexible, sensitive and will hold on to energies, albeit only for a short period of time. Water does not like to be exposed, unless it is kept in some sort of dance-like motion naturally. If you have water that is constantly kept flowing, for example, it is ok for it to be exposed. Otherwise, water should always be underground, in a tank or in a closed, opaque container.

Water doesn't care about the material in which it lives, but it's obviously better tasting when it's not in plastic or something that leaches chemicals into it, like limestone. Accordingly, it's best if you use some kind of Earthy material like wood, metal or stone to hold water.

Do not ever store water for more than a few hours at a time. A good way to think about this is to fill your container for a specific situation or engagement, throw away the remaining water after that situation has passed, and refill it for the next situation. For example, if you have many meetings in a day, do not fill a huge water bottle and carry it around all day, drinking from it all the time. Carry only what you need for one meeting, empty whatever's left and fill it again for the next meeting. If you go to the gym, fill your bottle with just enough water to hydrate you through your workout, then empty the rest before you leave. Understand that water in every situation picks up whatever's in that situation, so reusing water from one situation in another is a bad idea. When you throw away the little bit of water that is remaining, it takes away a lot of the negativity in the situation you were in, as well as some of the negativity that you released into the water unknowingly.

However, don't waste water. You should be throwing away maybe one mouthful of water at a time, not emptying liters of it every time you refill. And whenever you do empty the water, do so gratefully, knowing that the water is carrying some of what you would have had to absorb.

This also means that you should not be storing a huge amount of water, say in a pitcher in your kitchen, but refilling it as needed. Some people have a horrible habit of filling many bottles with water and sticking them in a fridge for later. All that will do is accumulate sickness for you to drink later. Use water as needed, store it at most for a few hours and empty whatever's remaining.

HOW MUCH TO DRINK

I hope this is obvious, but you should drink as much as you need, if not a bit more. My experience with people in the US is that they drink way too little water, and way too much of whatever else in the form of drinks, alcohol, smoothies and what not. In my home, you will not find anything but milk and room temperature water to drink. If you want to cleanse the body, you must drink a lot of water, but it's best not to keep sipping all day. Water is best consumed in bigger quantities occasionally, allowing the body time to process it, instead of sipping it all the time.

The healthier your body gets, the more it will prefer water over food, drinks, supplements and so on. Your body is absolutely phenomenal at making use of every little thing it finds both in the food you eat and in the environment you are in, but it needs water to distribute whatever it creates throughout the body. In most cases, when I see people wanting something to eat that is sweet and sugary, it is usually the body wanting to cool down, meaning that it just wants water and some shade at best. Instead of constantly snacking, experiment with drinking more water instead and see if it works for you.

THE BEST WATER FOR DRINKING

Your body will adjust to any source of drinking water you choose, as long as it's consistent. This means that if you like the tap water in your city, just make sure to carry tap water from your own home wherever you go instead of drinking water from all kinds of sources. If you use a specific filter, stick with it. Be consistent and as strict as possible when it comes to your preferred source of water, because while water from different sources may be "chemically" similar, it behaves differently depending on the source, how it's brought to you and so on.

Accordingly, commercial bottled water is literally the worst thing you can drink. Not only is commercial bottled water not always bottled at some pure spring, it is stored in transparent containers, transported in a rough manner and then stored in horrible places where all kinds of energies are swirling around, like a gas station or a grocery store. If you really must have commercial bottled water, first of all, stick to one kind and second, make sure to give the water time to settle before you drink it. When I was in Los Angeles, I sometimes had no choice but to buy bottled water and I would literally sit for at least 30 minutes with the water in the sunshine before I would drink it. Now, not all cities are as dirty as LA, but in general, unless you are receiving water directly from a pure natural source like a spring, river or a waterfall, you must give water at least 30 minutes to settle down in an opaque container before you drink it or leave it in the sun for 30 minutes if the container is transparent.

If you have excellent energy, which will happen if you make significant progress along the spiritual path, you will find water easier to purify simply by holding it for a while, shaking it gently and so on. Your body will do this naturally at some point if you make a lot of progress.

Of all the kinds of water sold commercially, sparkling water is better for you than plain water. Allow the fizz to leave—it carries away a lot of bad information—and then consume it. This is especially true in restaurants, where water is often served in a glass. If you can, drink sparkling water instead of plain water. However, avoid flavored water at all costs—it is bad for you. Water is not food, and the body responds *very* differently when it doesn't encounter plain water. Do not confuse the senses. Let the body enjoy some refreshing water and use it properly instead of working hard to figure out what it's been given.

The temperature of water makes a significant difference as to how it behaves inside you. While it is common and somewhat fashionable to drink cold or iced water nowadays, the best water is one that is at room temperature. If your insides are at a particular temperature, and you dump a whole bunch of water into it at a completely different temperature, your body is shocked and must recover from it, which is not a good idea. If you're wondering what all these athletes who compete in the Olympics are doing, where they drink cold water, have sugary, caffeinated drinks or use ice bags to cool down the body, they are torturing the body and pushing it into unnatural places to win or perform at a level most human bodies will not perform naturally. There is nothing good to be gained from the way some of these people live. If you want to grow more intelligent, then stop trying to force nature just so you can perform on a stage.

Understand that walking the spiritual path means walking without support, so the things that the world has decided are acceptable or even "good," are not going to be a part of your life. You will not be a "tea drinker," a "coffee addict" or a "wine aficionado." You will drink water and other naturally occurring substances, if necessary, like milk, coconut water and so on. That said, *while* you are on the path, your body will sometimes need all kinds of garbage to balance and re-balance itself as you make progress. At those times you may find yourself consuming all sorts of stuff that's available in the world. I will cover that in the chapter on food.

WATER FOR PAIN RELEASE

Of all the ways by which the body can release pain, contact with water is the best. Unlike normal pain release methods which require you to experience pain as it's leaving you, water can take away pain from your energy body and the physical body without you having to experience it on the way out. If you regularly experience lots of pain, upping your water intake is a fantastic way of giving your body the best chance of recovery. But when it comes to pain release, bathing in water is even more effective.

Recall the motorcycle accident I told you about that I had in Los Angeles? When that happened, I experienced a lot of pain, leaving me instantly at the moment I hit the ground. However, there was still pain inside that I had to release later to be completely healed. This pain didn't manifest on the outside, in that I didn't always feel it, but it was there nonetheless and affecting my daily life, slowing me down, limiting my range of motion and so on. My body refused all the advice, prescription medications and even the crutches the hospital gave me (I threw them away on the way out of the hospital or as soon as I reached home) and instead, embarked on what I can only describe as a two-month healing program. Every morning, I would take a bus from downtown LA all the way to Santa Monica, where I would spend 8 hours a day swimming in the ocean, walking around on the beach or lying in the sand. These 8 hours were sometimes sprinkled with activities like making sand sculptures, taking mud baths and other physical endeavors all designed to bring me in touch with the Earth. During those two months, my diet consisted almost exclusively of whole milk and water.

My body recovered miraculously because of this work without consuming any medication. Parts of my body were out of alignment after the accident, and they all snapped back into place over time. Even the scars on my skin disappeared and a lot of the angst I was feeling in LA thanks to witnessing the suffering of young women in the city was simply washed away in the sunshine. It is at the end of this two-month period that I started writing hundreds of pages of wisdom (and throwing all of it away), in preparation for writing this guide.

THE BEST WATER FOR HEALING

Hands down, the oceans contain the best water for healing. Nothing even comes close. There is a good reason the oceans are called the womb of the Earth, and if you spend any significant amount of time swimming in the oceans, you'll understand why. Unfortunately, our beaches are full of idiots who will constantly throw negative attention in your direction, especially if you are a young woman, so unless you are willing to do all that I did (drink milk, roast in the sun and stay active non-stop), you will end up receiving more negativity on the beach than you will release. In other words, my 8 hours at the beach every day were physically *extremely uncomfortable*. I was cold, tired and hungry all the time and that's what allowed me to heal the way I did.

The next best water for healing is found in rivers, but our rivers are quite polluted these days. Additionally, rivers are dangerous places and not for amateurs to simply jump into—most of you will get carried away and drown. I wouldn't recommend this unless you know what you are doing.

The next best are waterfalls. If you can find a nice private waterfall, good for you. Generally, they tend to be crowded and full of people behaving in an unruly manner. I wouldn't advise you to use them either.

Which brings me to the practice, and it requires only one thing: your bathtub.

THE PRACTICE

At least once every week, soak in your tub for at least 20 minutes without anything else to keep you occupied. This means no candles, bubbles, music, phone, books, people, incense—nothing but you and the water. You must be totally engaged with the water when you do this—don't simply fall asleep in the tub. You must play with the water, let it envelope you, perhaps use a tumbler or container to pour water over yourself repeatedly. The point of this practice is to give the water a chance to really touch you everywhere and for you to be focused entirely on the feeling of being healed as it does.

Remember, *anything* you do to make this experience more entertaining or comfortable will retard your progress. So, make sure it's just you and the water—nothing else.

EXCEPTIONS FOR MEN

This practice is not that important for men. You will gain the same benefit by taking a long shower. However, taking a 30-minute shower will waste a *lot* of water, so you're better off playing in the tub as well.

ADDITIONAL INSTRUCTIONS FOR WOMEN

The feminine has a very intimate relationship with water. When you do this practice, you are welcome to focus on the sensuousness of the experience, allowing it to take you wherever it goes. Don't be ashamed if it arouses you in some way—that's quite normal when women get in touch with water. You may find that being in the water for 20 minutes starts to release some memories and emotions. You are allowed to "take it out" on the water—it won't mind. Scream and shout if you like.

EXCEPTIONS FOR CHILDREN

Children don't "need" this, but if you have young children that want to be in the tub with you, let them. However, your focus must be *entirely* on the water, not your children. If you can't manage that, tell them to take a bath another time.

AFTER THE PRACTICE

This is extremely important. Once you are done with the water, you must let it drain. *Don't reuse the water.* Don't even look at it while it's draining if you can help it. You must dry yourself and *go straight to bed.* Don't read a book, don't pray and don't even say goodnight to your children or your partner. You must not engage in *any* activity after this practice, if you want to really benefit from it. This means that you must arrange for yourself to do this practice at the end of the week, after you're literally done with all your activities.

RESPECT WATER

The most important thing in life is love, and after love, the most import-ant thing is life itself, but after life, you must see water as the 3rd most important thing. It's *that* significant—more significant than your "significant other," your children, God, whatever. Wherever you go, water must make you smile, even if it's a puddle on the street. You must welcome it, cherish it, be in love with it and dance with it. Enjoy the rains on this planet (they're getting more frequent in some places!), go outside and dance in the storm if you like, let yourself be thrown around by the waves on a beach, give yourself a chance to get drenched on a bicycle, even take advantage of your neighborhood pool.

Understand this: the elements, like water, are not just physical. Yes, you can experience them after the physical body dies, but to experience water in full flow on this Earth is nothing short of magical. It's a privilege you must not take lightly. However, remember not to get caught up in activism and such nonsense—you're not here to save the Earth or the world. If you do see others disrespecting water, just leave if you cannot ignore it.

FOOD

When I first started receiving insights about food, I was surprised that people needed instructions on what to eat and how to eat, but this is what our civilization has come to. There are people on the planet now that are so sick that they cannot eat food—even good food—and need all kinds of help staying alive. Far from being a happy, pleasurable experience that you get to repeat all life long, food has become a source of great worry for some and for others, a chore—something they have to plan for and work hard at. On the path of light, you will not worry about food, because you will understand as you go that in fact your body is asking for the right stuff every moment—yes, even when it wants caffeine, sugar and fried food. I will help you understand what's really going on here and as your understanding and practices evolve, you will automatically come back to a place of good health and start to enjoy food again.

FOOD IS A NEED

It sounds obvious, but for many this isn't true. Many people now see food as an *opportunity* of some sort—an opportunity to be creative, to celebrate, to share, to have fun with and so on. This isn't a recent development but has been going on for a very long time. Under the guise of culture, tradition and so on, a great many things have been introduced into the consciousness of human beings and labeled as food. However, both the practice of seeing food as a sort of cultural opportunity and the resultant substances that have been introduced are all a consequence of sickness in the energy system. These illnesses have continued for so long that society and culture have accepted them as being normal in some way, but there is nothing normal about craving flavor, variety, excitement or any of the things that people are so enamored with when it comes to food.

There is only one reason your body consumes food, and that is to stay balanced on this Earth. The body needs energy and material, and it gets them both in the form of food. Everything else that is being added to food, including spices, seasonings, colors, textures (other than whatever is present naturally), means of processing, presentation and what not are all either a result of your energy system going out of whack and wanting all these things to stay balanced or a consequence of your psychology ruling over your body. Food is about fueling the body and ensuring it has what it needs to rebuild itself. Whatever else you are layering on top in terms of expectations and narratives is going to make you sicker and hold you back from making progress in your spiritual endeavor.

As your body heals and makes progress on the spiritual path, it will steadily become less and less tolerant of anything that isn't strictly food. Things like sugar, for example, will become a rarity and not something you take for granted in every meal. You will stop wanting spices and seasonings and start preferring the natural taste of food. You will stop consuming anything that is processed and go back to eating only what comes out of the ground or whatever has life in it, including the flesh of other animals. You will not want anything that is tainted in any way and go to some lengths to make sure the food you eat is pure. And all this will lead to a situation where all your desires, cravings and fantasies around food will end, you will come back to normal and have a perfect relationship with food.

I am not telling you this to dissuade you from the spiritual path. After all, many of you are *addicted* to finding new flavors and run around your city trying to find new ones. I am telling you this because many of you have absolutely no idea just how far you have pushed the body into unnatural states where you don't even know what real food tastes like. Once you start walking the path of light and all the bad information in every layer of your body starts to leave you, your palate will change—sometimes drastically, sometimes overnight. You must be willing to go along with this process. Don't worry—you'll still be able to enjoy the foods you used to, but at some point, your body will simply not want them. It will prefer to find the best of what life has to offer, and that goes for food as well. All this has to do with how food works and why your body chooses the foods it does.

HOW FOOD WORKS

The mechanism by which food works has been grossly misunderstood, thanks to a limited point of view that does not see how the energy system and the spiritual side of life function.

Food does not *give* you energy. Food is a *carrier* of energy and information into the body, but the source of that energy is you. You, the spirit, have the power to infuse what you love with energy, and it is that energy that is then transferred to whatever consumes it. Eating *well* means loving the food you eat. If you love the food you eat, it receives energy from you and transfers it into the body. If you don't enjoy the food you eat, it is literally wasted, and over time, eating poorly will make you very sick, weak, fat and so on. So, much more important than what you eat, is how you eat. Love the food you eat, or better not eat at all!

The material present in the food serves two functions: one, it is used to repair, replenish and rebuild the body, and two, it carries the energy you have infused it with. Different substances carry energy into the body to different extents. For example, water is a very efficient carrier of energy, as are salt and sugar. Fat, in general, is a very poor carrier of energy, while whole grains are amazing at the same thing.

Understand that food doesn't affect just the physical body, but also the psyche (if you have one) as well as the energy system. Different substances can have an enormous impact on your balance even if they don't carry any energy into the system. For example, honey will drastically increase the heat inside your body, which is why it is often found in lozenges, some kinds of cold medications and so on. In these cases, it is the honey that's helping you heal, while the pharmaceutical is mostly just there to provide comfort.

In the same manner that the energy you receive from people directly must be processed, filtered and eliminated of all the bad information in it so you can stay healthy, your body needs to process, filter and eliminate the garbage in the food you eat. This would not be a big issue if all the food you ate was untouched by anyone else, but in our global supply chain system, *all* the food we eat is handled by many people and their energy makes its way to the food you eat in greater or smaller amounts. This means that your body has to work quite hard to get rid of the bad information no matter what you're consuming, and this is made much worse if you eat processed foods, prepared foods or simply eat out a lot.

When you are sick or depressed and your energy level is low, you will not be able to eat because your body will not receive the energy necessary to use the food you put into your system as well as eliminate the garbage effectively. In fact, people who are generally not feeling well tend to consume sugar precisely because they need something that will carry the most amount of energy into the body without requiring much effort to process it. And if the sickness is too severe, they'll shift to something even subtler, like water, soup and such. Nobody wants to eat steak when they're feeling sick.

ELIMINATION IS PARAMOUNT

While we are on the subject, a note on elimination. My experience among young people in the US is that they hold on to too much trash in their system for way too long. If you start to make progress on the spiritual path, you will no longer be one of them. Your body will actively make you cleanse, which means it will start to drink more water, eat more fruit and add more fiber into your diet—it will simply do this without you having to ask. And when that starts, be prepared for a long period of cleansing, which is anything but pleasant while it's happening.

I don't want you to underestimate the impact that the process of true healing will have on your lifestyle. Picture a smooth bullet train riding on tracks, hardly making a sound. Now picture a dirty, polluting, noisy, rattling, screeching diesel engine covered in soot, grime and garbage. The bullet train happens at the end, once you are enlightened. Along the way, you'll be like that diesel engine. Every layer of your body will eliminate all the garbage you've accumulated so far, as well as all the garbage you're receiving, at an accelerated pace. You will go to the toilet more than once a day and sometimes even feel like taking multiple showers a day, especially if you work in a filthy environment (e.g., New York's Wall Street). Your energy body will throw oodles of bad information out, making some people not want to be around you anymore. You may start swearing, ranting and raving at times and not exactly be seen as the life of the party. Your neighbors might have to buy earplugs just so they can find relief from all your pooping, farting, hacking, coughing, chortling, snoring—you name it! I am happy that working from home is becoming more acceptable—use it to your advantage. This is one more reason you need to be seriously committed to the path of light to finish, because it is not pleasant, even for your neighbors sometimes. The question you must always ask yourself is: do you really want to finish?

By the way, if, during this time, you go to any usual doctor and tell them how you live, they'll probably think you're sick and prescribe you medication to stop you from "cleansing" as much. It's up to you if you want to intervene in what is a natural process of healing, just so you can look better, feel better temporarily, or maybe survive a disease that might kill you on the way out.

Now that we've gotten that out of the way, let's get back to food.

HOW TO EAT

What all this means for you is that you must eat when you're energetic and healthy, not when you are sick. And you must ensure that you have sufficient interest in the food before you sit down to eat, i.e., don't simply eat because "it's time." If you really want to get the best out of food, you must be ravenously hungry when you sit down to eat. I say this because what I've observed all over the United States is that our young people eat poorly, i.e., they eat garbage, with little interest, and woefully little amounts of food. Let me share with you a story.

When I was working very hard both spiritually as well as in the world, I was in my late 20s and a student at Indiana University. The university had a fantastic gym and pool, and I would often use them on the weekends to stay in shape as best as I could. I would often go to the gym on Saturday mornings, then swim for an hour in the pool, maybe take a few dives off the high platforms and then be hungry beyond imagining. On days like these, I had no energy to cook, and the usual array of offerings in the restaurants wouldn't even come close to making me feel replenished. Luckily for me, there were several buffets in town that advertised 'All You Can Eat' lunch specials for a low price. Now, it wasn't unusual at the time for me to eat several plates of food in one sitting no matter what day it was, but on this particular Saturday, I literally felt like everything I was eating was disappearing into a black hole inside me. By the time I finished eating an entire plate of food, it was as if I had just arrived at the restaurant. That day, I ate so much food—I remember eating 16 legs of tandoori chicken in addition to everything else—that I was quite impolitely asked to leave.

I am sure any professional bodybuilders reading this can relate—at least when it comes to the quantity of food—but at the time I wasn't muscular or fat, but somewhat normal in size. It's just that the amount of spiritual work I was doing was consuming most of what I ate, with my physical body receiving the scraps, so to speak.

As young people, you should be doing *tons* of spiritual work just for yourselves, figuring out how life works, building your energy system, coming to an understanding of what you really need in life and who you are, not to mention *also* building up your physicality, making it strong, resilient and able to handle just about anything thrown at you by life. This means that you should be eating gobs of food at every meal. Restaurants all over the world should be frightened of teenagers and young people in general. Instead, kids and young people alike are being force-fed enormous quantities of sugar, fillers, "refined" foods and of course, alcohol as soon as they're able. None of those things will help you build a good life, nor will they give you the strength you need to withstand life's vicissitudes.

The lesson for you is this: as a young person, if you are unable to eat obnoxious quantities of food (by most people's standards), there is something wrong with your energy system. Most of the food out there is not dense or nutritious anymore, which means you really need to up your intake significantly (and eliminate accordingly!) in order to be healthy. If you are unable to do this, either your energy is being blocked by bad information from functioning well, or it is just low because you've spent most of your energy on worthless pursuits. Either way, understand this much: you must never worry about eating too much, especially when it comes to good food. When you get moving in earnest on the spiritual path, you will sometimes consume enough food to put a dairy cow to shame.

WHAT TO EAT

Good food is really hard to come by these days, *unless* you're cooking for yourself. Cooking is a fundamental life skill that you *must* acquire early on because it will make probably the biggest difference in your health overall. The food served by other people (yes, even your parents) is chock full of garbage that they've picked up all over the world and your body is going to waste a lot of energy trying to filter it all out. So, first things first, try and ensure that the food you are eating is as minimally handled by other people as possible.

This eliminates most of what is on the shelves in grocery stores, at least in the United States, because you'll have to stick with fresh fruits, vegetables, milk, meat, eggs, whole grains—you get the idea. Anything processed is going to make you sick, *but* that doesn't mean they don't have a role to play.

The way your body functions is like this: if you are already out of balance, your body will *first* want to bring you back into balance before addressing whatever problem it is you are dealing with. It will not try to solve problems while you are off kilter. It is as if you are walking on a tightrope and you are about to fall--your body will first find a counterweight so you can stay upright, and *then* it will figure out what to eliminate so that you can come back to balance without using the counterweight. This is basically what has happened all over the United States, and why there are so many products full of garbage on the shelves in our grocery stores. If you are already sick inside (even only at an energy level), it's as if your foundation is tilted to one side, causing your body to also tilt with it. To correct the imbalance, your body will *force* you to eat trash so that it can find a counterweight to help you come back to balance. This is often in the form of refined foods, sugary foods, spicy foods, alcohol, chocolate, candy—basically all the stuff in the grocery store that doesn't look like food at all (at least I don't see them as food). If you continue to push the body forward instead of giving it time to heal, your body will become dependent on these kinds of substances just to carry on. It will keep finding even more trash in the future to keep itself balanced.

It is for this reason that so many things that are not food have become acceptable for cultures around the world to eat. And of course, now the problem is so acute that pharmaceuticals have joined the fray. All of this is just a side effect of being very sick at every level and being unable to heal. Addictions quickly follow once a state of imbalance is reached, and many people have totally given up trying to come back to balance. Just witness how many people in the US are *totally* dependent on caffeine just to make it through their morning.

Once your body is in perfect balance, it will not even want the *smell* of bad food. Even things like cheese, hot chili peppers, garlic, chips, fruit smoothies, beer and wine will become difficult for you to tolerate. None of those things count as food as far as I am concerned, but they can be used in miniscule quantities as medicine occasionally. In fact, as you progress on the path of light, you'll be quite surprised as to how few things your body will consider to be acceptable food.

By the way, there's no problem with you eating meat of any kind. The body must work much harder when trying to filter out the garbage in meat, which is why it's not recommended for people trying to walk the spiritual path. However, when you are serious on the spiritual path in the world in which we live, there will be times when only meat will give you the amount of material you need to rebuild your system. Accept it.

I could write an entire book on the subject of substances and how they affect every single layer of the body, but it is useless wisdom from my point of view, because your body will find its own way as it goes, and you won't need to refer to guidance. In fact, I would encourage you to stop reading all these idiotic narratives that have emerged of late as to why certain kinds of foods are bad for you—carbohydrates, for example. Anyone who works hard physically knows that absolutely nothing will fuel the body like good whole-grain carbohydrates will—and keep you going for a long time. If your body wants to eat a pound of cooked rice with a side of potatoes and some meat in every meal, so what? Don't worry so much about all this popular "wisdom," which is based on a faulty understanding of how life is progressing on this Earth. At the end of the day, if you go to your deathbed and can honestly say to yourself that you ate whatever the hell you wanted every moment of your life, you will be very happy even if nothing else went well.

The fundamental lesson for you is this: when you are healthy, your body will eat better food. You must *be well* to *eat well*, not the other way round. The practices in this book are all designed to bring you back into balance, restore the flow of energy, and raise your intelligence so that you see the world more clearly. Only when bad information starts to leave you at an accelerated rate will your lifestyle—including your food preferences—change.

So, no matter how you look, how you feel, what you eat and how much you eat, stop judging your food habits, because they're simply a response to your current state of balance and not a sin. Just practice what I've laid out in this book and let things evolve as they will.

PREFER COOKED FOOD

There is no question that the best food for a human being is raw, unprocessed food. However, you will not be able to find pure, raw, unprocessed food at a reasonable price anywhere in the world at this point, simply because even the soil, the air and the water are so polluted. Combine this with the numbers of people that handle food at every turn, and you are basically out of luck when it comes to living a healthy lifestyle solely on raw food. Those who eat mostly raw food (and I've met a few) are severely out of balance and simply don't know it most of the time. I don't want you to be one of them.

Cooking removes a great number of impurities from the food, especially impurities of the energetic kind, aka bad information. No matter how many people handle a bag of rice, if you cook it fully, you will not have to eat their garbage—guaranteed. You can happily eat cooked rice, pasta, roasted potatoes, steamed vegetables, deep fried chicken, etc. all day long without worrying about energetic impurities because those kinds of cooking remove all of it. So, as far as possible, prefer cooked food to raw food, even if it is just gently steamed. And of course, it's always best if you cook for yourself, *unless you are a woman.*

There is something women need to be aware of when it comes to cooking: as a woman, you must never cook for anyone but yourself and your prepubescent children. Most of you are so low on energy nowadays—I've met so many of you that are in deep depression, often without realizing it—that you *cannot* afford to give away even an ounce of your energy to anyone or anything except your own life. Additionally, as a woman, it is your privilege to receive energy from others and create something beautiful with it, so you must use this ability for good.

What this means is that if you have a male partner, *they* should be the cook, for you and your children. You can help embellish the food if you like, or help in other ways like helping with cleaning up, setting the table, etc. You are even welcome to buy your partner cookbooks, tools, whatever you think will help him in the kitchen. However, at the end of the day, he must be the cook. He needs to put his heart into the cooking process. The power that flows out of his heart will make it into food and help you and your children grow stronger.

Once your children reach teenage years, they should get involved in the cooking as well, especially boys. They will develop a fantastic skill that will serve them well into old age, plus they will learn about food and generally become better people as a result, but most importantly, you will not be drained of the energy you need. Why this is so will become clearer in the chapters on feminine power, but for now remember this much: a man's place is in the kitchen. Let him cook!

There is something else that this specific division of labor accomplishes though, which is related to a deep and important topic covered in the next chapter.

GROUNDING

Grounding is such an important topic, and one so easily achieved, that I find it incredulous that so many people are suffering from the lack of it. In this chapter I will cover in detail what grounding is, what happens when it's not present, how to achieve it, how to maintain it and most importantly, how all of civilization is actively supporting your ability to ground yourself even though you don't realize it or know how to take advantage of it.

WHAT GROUNDING MEANS

When people talk about being "grounded," they are usually referring to coming back to reality in some way, although most people's idea of reality itself is flawed. For example, money isn't real, and neither is your gender identity. Grounding simply means that you are stable no matter what is going on in your life, and stability means that you can clearly separate reality from non-reality even if you are not feeling 100% well. I am sure many of you have experienced what it's like to have too much alcohol in your system and how it warps your sense of what is socially acceptable. However, if you are stable, even after drinking, you will not behave inappropriately from an existential point of view, i.e., you will not do things like harass people, hurt them, get into dangerous situations and so on.

The way your existence functions on this Earth requires that you be at a certain level of energy that is neither too high, nor too low. If your energy is too low, you will become depressed, life will seem dull or lonely and you will lack clarity as to what to do, where to go, how to be, etc. If your energy is too high, you will hallucinate and cook up all kinds of wild narratives, like the kind you hear from so-called "conspiracy theorists," "ghost hunters" and such. You must be in the middle and the middle isn't a point, but a pretty wide range. Regardless of where you are energetically, it is grounding that ensures that you don't leave the body and go flying around, which is what some yogis do. As a human being though, you didn't come here to fly, but to enjoy an Earthly existence, so it's important that you always stay grounded.

The root of your energy body lies pretty much at the base of your spine and that is where you must always be grounded. This isn't something you have to "try" to do—it's natural for your body to be grounded in this manner. From here, your energy can be made to rise to different points, changing your life experience when it does. Some of you probably are starting to think about "chakras" and such at this point, but I am not going to talk about them at all, because they are not useful for any of you. All this unnecessary "knowledge" has only caused idiots to start writing books about yoga without truly understanding what it's all about, and I am not going to encourage that any further.

From the standpoint of "feeling," grounding feels like you are planted on the ground, not something you feel in your spine. The heaviness that you feel when you pay attention to your body is a consequence of grounding, not gravity. If I raised your energy to a certain point, you would feel, and behave, as if you are totally weightless—a very dangerous condition that sometimes happens to people on the spiritual path, but thankfully only under the supervision of powerful yogis who are in charge of the situation. I have no interest in such miracles though.

WHAT HAPPENS WHEN YOU ARE UNGROUNDED

First, when you are ungrounded, your vision is affected to some extent, even if you aren't totally conscious of it. You will feel that things are not quite right. Things around you may become hazy, dream-like or just more "magical" in some way. There are people who intentionally poison themselves using hallucinogens and drugs of all kinds to experience this, not realizing that it permanently damages your energy system if not brought under control quickly enough. To give you an analogy, being ungrounded means that you have more electricity surging through a wire than it can handle—at some point it will burn out like an overheated filament in a light bulb.

Another important change that happens is a feeling of weightlessness, and the strength of this feeling depends on the individual. Usually, heavier individuals don't experience this as much as very slim ones. Women, especially, are quite susceptible to feeling this way. Unfortunately, many of them think this is a good thing. It is not.

The most significant effect of being ungrounded is that it brings you in touch with your subconscious, which, in the case of *all* of you, is in a state of utter chaos. The subconscious is where all the inputs, experiences, bad information—everything—is being actively processed, filtered and eliminated. Most of you have way too much garbage in your system, much more than you can possibly work out in a single lifetime unless you committedly follow all the practices I've laid out in this book. So, when you come in touch with your subconscious, suddenly everything goes nuts. You may start talking to people who aren't here, "having experiences" that aren't real, seeing things that aren't present, hearing voices and sounds, making connections between objects in a way that makes absolutely no sense and is wrong, etc. You start to encounter bits and pieces of possible futures mixed with ideas, emotions and experiences of the past and all of it becomes a horrible soup that you start swimming in without having any control.

Nearly 100% of the "conditions" that people refer to as "mental illness," are simply due to a lack of grounding, and nothing else. These "conditions" don't need pharmaceuticals, but a change of lifestyle, a slow deconditioning of the body so that it can give up some of the garbage it has accumulated, and a lifestyle that is more in touch with the ground (literally the Earth) than before. Most people are unwilling to make such simple changes to their lifestyles to be healthy though, because it would require them to give up some of their most cherished obsessions, memories, addictions and such. As a result, people continue to suffer, burn out and often commit suicide in hopes of finding a way out of the chaos. As I've stated before, suicide doesn't work, so if you are experiencing mental illness and want to get past it, you must start grounding yourself a bit more consciously.

Grounding won't interfere with any treatments or therapies you are currently using. In fact, if you ground yourself well, you may find yourself getting rid of some of the drugs and treatments you are using today. You are welcome to use grounding in addition to whatever else you may be doing today to help yourself, but don't be an idiot and throw away your support mechanisms willy-nilly. Like everything on the path of light, things will happen to you as necessary—you don't have to force changes.

GROUNDING IS EASY

Unfortunately, our universe—and all of creation—is rising in energy. This is unfortunate only from a grounding perspective, because when energy rises, so does intelligence, which is exactly what we all need. If we didn't have the Earth to keep us grounded, none of us would exist, but this is exactly why it is so easy to ground yourself. In order to ground yourself, all you must do is come back to the Earth and stay in touch with it *physically* until you are stable again.

Next time you are too anxious, worried, excited, overjoyed, going crazy, feeling woozy or experiencing any kind of "strangeness" (this latter feeling is common in big cities), find a patch of bare Earth, take off your shoes and stand on it. If you need even more support, sit down on the ground without your shoes and make sure both your palms and your feet touch the Earth in some way. *Do not lie down on the ground*, because when you do, you are most likely to look up at the sky and that will severely unground you. It's best that you simply sit down on the ground and keep your eyes open.

This works even if you are a concrete sidewalk or flooring made of natural materials if it's in touch with the Earth and is at ground level. Don't expect this to work if you are on some high floor inside a tall building. Yes, in fact there is power surging through your energy system that requires grounding just like our electrical supply at home does and getting in touch with the ground does almost the same thing as grounding an electrical wire. We weren't made to be so out-of-touch with the Earth for such long periods of time. Too many people in the US never walk barefoot anymore, anywhere and this is a huge reason why there is so much insanity (even the mild kind) all over the country. People have simply lost touch with reality and literally so!

Specifically, the Earth and Water are grounding elements, while the other elements will generally not help you as much. In fact, Wind will usually make you more anxious than you are, Fire will cause you to raise your energy too much, and the Sky will unground you severely and possibly make you lose consciousness. If you are in sufficient contact with both Water and Earth every day, you will not struggle to stay grounded.

FOOD AND DRINK

Almost all food and drink is essentially grounding in nature, which means the simple act of eating and drinking should be keeping people grounded. If so, why is there still such a problem? Because people are constantly consuming substances that are causing them to lose the benefits of the very food and drink they are consuming. For instance, caffeine, most pharmaceuticals, cigarettes, marijuana and other drugs, excessively spicy foods, hot chili peppers, excessive use of ingredients that activate the body such as onion and garlic—all these are ungrounding, meaning that if they are a part of your life, you will need some extra support to stay grounded well. Some things like garlic are good as medication or as "boosters" for the digestive system occasionally and others like caffeine are harmful to the body. When you start to come back to balance, all those substances (plus alcohol and other depressants like excessive sugar) will simply disappear from your life.

If you are struggling with mental illness, the last thing you need to do is go on a diet! You must eat and eat whatever the hell your body wants to eat. If you want a slice of cheesecake every day, fine. Don't judge yourself, but at the same time, make sure to practice what's in this book so you recover from any harmful effects of your current eating habits. By the way, all the practices in this book will work regardless of the medications you are taking. In fact, many of you will throw away your medications when you start to make some progress.

There are certain surprising things though that are quite grounding and good to reach for in a jiffy. These include *decaf* coffee (the more bitter the better!), sugar, carbonation (especially plain carbonated water), soda (the caffeine-free variety), heavy foods (like beef, cheese and bread), yellow foods (e.g., bananas), salty and deep-fried foods (like fried potatoes) and extremely sour stuff (like candy, lemonade or tamarind). Put some of these together and you'll see what we've done as a civilization to compensate for the lack of proper grounding: fast food, which consists of sodas, fries, burgers, desserts and the like. Unfortunately, most fast food is stupid, in the sense that it is out of balance. There's no need for excessive sugar, salt, caffeine, fillers or the associated stupidity that comes with the culture of fast food, in the form of plastics, "drive-throughs" and other things that are going to do the opposite of keeping you grounded.

Instead, make a nice pizza at home with whole grains, olive oil, fresh cheese (not the processed variety), fresh veggies, serve it with some homemade sparkling lemonade and you'll have a tasty, healthy meal that is also extremely grounding for you. You can even have fries with that.

If you know how to use all the food in the world to your advantage, you can benefit, as I did when I was motorcycling around the United States, needing constant grounding thanks to relentless exposure to wind and sunlight and using fast food to help myself. However, my food habits are under the control of the Divine Feminine, so I cannot give you a formula to help you choose the right foods. Only when your intelligence rises will your body know how to use food to keep you grounded.

TEXTURE

The United States isn't as bad as Europe when it comes to the lack of texture in modern daily life, but it is getting there. Texture is extremely important, because your senses will keep you grounded. You must come in touch with the rough stuff: the sharp, the spiky, the coarse, the rocky, etc. If you take a walk in the desert or a canyon, barefoot, you'll see what I mean. Pretty much everything you step on, touch or rub against will make its presence felt. There is no way you'll be worrying about finances when that's happening. You'll be totally grounded in reality.

This goes for clothing, objects and furniture—indeed everything.

Instead of going out and accumulating textured stuff, just learn to live without furniture in the home, use the floor as much as possible, wear natural materials as much as possible and stop wearing shoes all over the place. When you don't wear shoes and walk barefoot as much as possible, your feet will get enough of a workout that you won't have to cover them up for the sake of energy purity as I described in Chapter 12. But be wise—don't walk barefoot on the sidewalks and expect to get anything but sick.

WOMEN

Yes, believe it or not, women are exceptionally grounding—and most have no idea that they are. I am not talking about their flesh, which is grounding to some extent, especially for young babies who need all the grounding support they can find. Babies need to be in contact with their mother's flesh as much as possible—24 hours a day if they can manage it—because their energy isn't strong enough to keep them grounded. This is also true of young children, especially boys, who often just need a good strong hug (skin-to-skin) because they're unable to maintain balance all the time. If your kid is fidgety, see if a bit of grounding will take care of it instead of feeding them more pharmaceuticals!

But beyond flesh, it is *women*, specifically, that are grounding—meaning an elevated level of feminine energy. Boys, who often need a bit more grounding than girls, just need to be around women sometimes. They don't need to look at them, touch them and so on. If you know someone that is going nuts, often looking into a woman's eyes is enough to calm them down, assuming that the other woman herself isn't ungrounded! If you are a woman, this is an easy way to bring whatever heated argument you're having with your male partner to a quick end. Hold him close, have him look into your eyes and things will stabilize. Please don't do this to people you're not close to—it's extremely inappropriate!

This is one of the ways that the media, especially media that exposes women inappropriately, is being used by people to ground themselves. Such a thing wouldn't be necessary if people simply lived more in touch with the Earth, as opposed to looking for substitutes.

ACTIVITY

Activity can be very grounding, because stillness does the exact opposite. Fidgetiness, inability to pay attention, wanting to move around, wanting to rock or dance, etc. are all just ways in which the body is trying to rid itself of an elevated level of energy, which it can easily do with activity. Regular exercise, especially outdoors, can eliminate all need for pharmaceuticals used to treat mental illness in some cases. In fact, even regularly working out in a gym is useful, thanks to all the contact with heavy metal that it encourages. However, beware of engaging in activity when you are already too ungrounded—it will make you want to do crazy things like skydiving, racing on the streets, picking a fight with people, etc. Young men will often get into stupid pursuits like these because they are simply out of control at an energy level, not because they are genuinely interested in risky activities.

HEAT AND SUNSHINE

Living in cold weather is a bad idea if you are suffering with a mental illness of any sort, and living in a big city where you are surrounded by tall buildings with little sunshine is even worse. Your body needs sunshine daily, at the very least. And it needs warm weather to stay healthy because the fluids in your body will literally move more freely in warmer weather. Yes, recovery from physical illnesses like injuries is much better done in colder weather, but if you want to be healthy in general, you must live in warmer climates with more than enough sunshine to keep you grounded. While it is easier to exercise harder in cooler weather, only when there is sufficient energy in the atmosphere you live in will you feel replenished. The energy you need to replenish yourself doesn't necessarily have to come from sunshine only. Rain, thunderstorms, lightning storms and other severe weather events can suddenly raise your energy level without warning, allowing you to either replenish yourself, or suddenly become ungrounded. Excessive sunshine can also be ungrounding, but I've yet to see anyone in the US with so much energy that too much sunshine would cause them to go nuts.

If you cannot manage natural heat, artificial heat will work and so will wearing warm clothing, but nothing works like naturally warm weather.

Understand that your body responds to the weather as a whole, not just to temperature and humidity, for example. If the weather is warm and supportive, your whole system will flow better and you will find that you have sufficient energy throughout the day to accomplish whatever it is you want to do, including cleansing.

EXERCISE

It is a great thing to see that of all the many things that human beings should be doing regularly, at least exercise is getting enough recognition. Unfortunately, what most people consider exercise isn't exercise. There is a slight difference between what is being advertised as "working out" and what is considered "exercise." In this chapter, I will unpack the two and help you understand what you should do and how you should do it to stay healthy at all layers of the body.

WORKING OUT

Working out literally means that you have problems in the body at some layer that you need to "work out." Almost 100% of whatever is being conjured up these days under the guise of fitness helps you work out, and not necessarily get healthier, especially when it comes to aggressive techniques.

The main reason people need to work out is that everyone is consuming an elevated level of bad information simply by living in civilization. Unless you're totally covered up, your body picks up almost everything in its environment, absorbs it and then must eliminate it in some way. What you do when you work out is literally *push* energy out of the body, because information cannot be eliminated all by itself. Whenever you eliminate information, it must be packaged in energy and then thrown out. This means that the process of cleansing releases a whole bunch of energy along with the bad information associated with it.

Whenever you have excess amounts of garbage in your system, you will feel aggressive in some manner, either physically, psychologically or emotionally. There is nothing you can do about that feeling, except give in and push all that energy out so that the aggression can leave you. If you work out on a regular basis, and work out sufficiently, you will not be aggressive the rest of the time. This is the real benefit of working out—your insanity and madness leave you before you do something stupid or take it out on someone or something else.

HOW MUCH TO WORK OUT

It is for this reason that working out *always* involves something that taxes your system significantly. Don't think that you can do some simple stretches or gentle water aerobics and get by. You must work out *hard* and it's extremely important that you feel like you've been hit by a train at the end of it. In other words, you shouldn't have much left to give at the end of your workout. This is a situation you will not be able to get to on day one, especially if you haven't seriously worked out in a while, but you will have to get there if you want the benefit.

I tend to work out in the gym 6 days a week, every morning, and it always involves lifting heavy weights. Usually, at the end of my workout, I am unable to lift even 5 pounds of weight and there are days when I find myself drifting off to sleep on the bench due to sheer exhaustion. *However,* thanks to the fact that I live with zero issues, my body recovers extremely quickly. I don't even experience any soreness during the day because the natural state of my body is to be at rest and not agitated. You will not be at this level unless you make significant progress in your cleansing. The cleaner your system is, the better everything functions, and you will find that your workouts are a lot easier to sustain without consuming steroids, vitamins, electrolytes, supplements, caffeine, protein shakes or even excessive amounts of meat. None of those are part of my routine, plus I only eat twice a day. When you are clean, your body will use everything more efficiently.

There is one more factor that affects this greatly though and that is sleep, the subject of the next chapter.

I don't care what state you are in today. If you want to progress spiritually, you *must* work out 6 days a week, no compromises. Maybe you are only able to walk about half a mile today before you run out of breath and can barely stand—I was like this after my motorcycle accident in Los Angeles. But you must keep it up, day after day, 6 days a week, for the rest of your life. Otherwise, your body will not function properly.

Obviously, not everyone can manage a hard workout like this because it takes a lot of energy and strength—yet another reason few succeed on the path of light.

This whole idea that you need a rest day in between is absolute nonsense, invented by people who work out excessively, don't rest enough during the day and don't sleep enough at night. Sure, you shouldn't work out the *same* part of the body until it's recovered, but you must work out! You're taking in enough garbage daily to need it.

By the way, I hope it's obvious that a workout should always be in a very well-ventilated environment, because everyone that is working out is *literally* throwing out their garbage. Never work out in a cramped environment with lots of people, or in a space that doesn't get enough fresh air and natural light (air conditioning and fluorescent lights are not acceptable substitutes) because if you do, you'll get sick.

NUTRITION FOR WORKOUTS

Do not, ever, workout on an empty stomach, or while hungry. This is not your traditional Hatha Yoga, which requires that you be empty when you do it, because we're not trying to do the same thing here. This is working out hard in the gym or elsewhere, actively stressing your body and pushing your garbage out. It takes *enormous* amounts of energy to accomplish this, and you must be fueled properly or you run the risk of injury or even death if you are too weak.

The only thing that can really fuel a good workout are carbohydrates.

Adding a little bit of fat is fine, but protein isn't necessary—you can have that after if you want. Almost all good food, including whole grains, have sufficient protein for most people (e.g., whole wheat contains about 13%) so eating some good whole grains at least 30 minutes before a workout (so that your body has time to digest it), is essential. It is a bad idea to eat in the middle of workouts—these kinds of tactics have been invented by people pushing their bodies into unnatural states, like professional bodybuilders, or Olympic athletes. Eat properly, let yourself feel the energy kick in and then focus entirely on the workout. Drinking water during a workout is ok, but don't fool your body into thinking more food is coming by drinking sports drinks or something with flavor or sugar in it.

SLOW DOWN

I've experienced something called High Intensity Interval Training, which involves short periods of extremely intense activity followed by a bit of rest, rinse and repeat. *Intensity* does not mean *speed*, which is unfortunately how many studios are interpreting this. You can work out intensely by lifting weights very slowly and in a controlled manner. You can also workout intensely by steadily climbing a hill at a slow pace, bicycling up a gentle incline at a steady rate, running at a pace where you can easily talk, etc. The point of a workout is to push as much energy out as possible, but not *as fast as possible*. Working out too fast is one of the reasons people don't work out enough—it's simply not sustainable. I'll cover more on why this is bad in the next chapter.

When you are thinking of a workout, visualize yourself as a giant river that is flowing smoothly, gently and powerfully. A river pushes a lot of water every second, but it doesn't do it like a pressure washer, which pushes not as much water, but does so at enormous pressure. If you like lifting weights, this means lifting at the edge of your capability but in a slow, controlled manner with good form. If you like running, pay attention to your posture and gait and perhaps run uphill if you're not being challenged enough. If you like to swim, use a full range of motion, breathe evenly and regularly and don't make the lifeguard nervous!

Most importantly, don't work out in a way your body doesn't want to.

Try different activities and see what your body naturally wants to do. For example, thanks to all the accidents I've had on a motorcycle, my body doesn't want anything to do with running now and prefers hiking, lifting weights and swimming even though as a child I preferred sprinting and athletics. Take your time and learn what your body really wants to do to give the most it can give during a workout.

Most of you need to change your expectations of how the body changes. It will not change at lightning speed, and any quick results you get are obtained at the cost of unbalancing your system in some way. If you push your system too fast, you may look good now, but you will pay for it at some point in your life. Your body *literally* moves at the speed of the Earth, i.e., at a geological pace, like a glacier (although even glaciers are moving too fast nowadays thanks to imbalances!). Do not expect to change your body in a matter of weeks or months. Just make working out a habit and forget about what the body does as a result—it will do what is necessary.

EXERCISE VS WORKING OUT

If all this is what a workout is, what is exercise? Exercise is when you are replenishing the body's energy stores by gently and slowly allowing your energy to flow into it. While a workout always depletes the body's energy stores, exercise rejuvenates it. Exercise is always done in a *very* gentle and slow manner. Examples of exercise include taking a walk at the beach or a stroll at the park, walking your dog, going for a nice bike ride around the neighborhood, splashing around a bit in your neighborhood pool or doing very gentle and slow laps, flying a kite, etc.

Your body doesn't need much exercise, but it will ask you for it sometimes or just naturally do it. You are welcome to exercise as and when you feel like it and it doesn't matter if you've been fed or not.

The most important thing about exercise is that it requires a peaceful environment. This is not the time for you to push, nor is it a good idea to exercise with other people. You must be in as pure an environment as you can be, *love* your body and allow it to rejuvenate itself.

Many people who often overeat misinterpret their body's signals because they've not had the time to really pay attention and see what the body is trying to say. If you are one of those people that isn't sure if you should be eating as much, just go exercise whenever you "feel like eating" and see if it reveals something you didn't know before. Understand that true hunger is *debilitating*—you will literally not want to do anything until you eat, whereas the body's need for exercise appears more often like an impulse. Remember, when your body wants exercise, it wants a pure environment— fresh air, sunshine, a nice breeze or even a gentle rain, things like that.

STRENGTH IS LIFE

I've noticed that people who are old (which has to do with energy, not physical age) and people who don't regularly workout often talk about something or the other being wrong with their body. My own life was like this when I was giving myself spiritually, as well as during my healing period because I was literally all out of energy and couldn't work out. Now, just because you work out doesn't mean that you'll avoid that cancer you've been worrying about—there's more to it that I'll share in the next chapter—but you certainly will not complain as much even if you do get it!

Ultimately, as a yogi named Swami Vivekananda was known to have said, "strength is life and weakness is death." I've heard so many people complain about so many different things about their body that are simply a result of them not working out and strengthening themselves, both phys-ically and spiritually. You must have the strength not only to do whatever you do on a day-to-day basis (e.g., carrying 30 lbs. of groceries in one hand while unlocking the door with the other), but also to contribute by creating something beautiful you care about. Plus, all the practices I've described in this book will take a lot more energy expenditure than you've ever had to experience and the only way to keep your energy levels up is to regularly clear out the garbage and allow good energy to fill it. When you do this properly, you will grow both physically and spiritually. Plus, growth contin-ues even after death!

EXCEPTIONS FOR WOMEN

There is something women need to understand about working out: a purely physical workout doesn't benefit you as much as it does the boys. Your system is much more refined, gentler and subtler in many ways, and it requires a different approach to working out than whatever the boys are up to. Sure, it is easier to just go do whatever they're all doing—lifting weights, running, bicycling, etc. but these will not help you grow.

Most of your garbage is at a different layer than the physical and energy layer—what I am calling the emotional layer. If you really want to get the most out of your life, you must workout not just physically, but also *creatively*. You are most welcome to continue going to the gym, doing Pilates, kickboxing, flying yoga or whatever, but you *must* add a creative component to your life or risk basically remaining weak in an area that is paramount to you functioning well as a woman.

Pick something that you love to be creative at, and when I say creative, I mean *truly creative*, in the sense that it forces you to envision something that doesn't yet exist, come up with a way of manifesting it that may not yet be there and making it happen. This does not have to be about inventing new products and services. In fact, there's nothing creative about whatever the world is doing in that sense, as I'll explain more in the chapter on feminine powers. It has everything to do with the *way* you go about doing something. Let me give you an example.

I like to play the piano when I have the energy to do so. I don't play anything other than classical music at this point, but my goal when playing the piano has absolutely nothing to do with playing *exactly* as the notation says. I don't insert my own notes or change the rhythm when I am playing someone else's composition, but I have a vision for how I want to express myself while playing a piece. I can play the same bar with the same notes in the same time signature in a million different ways, each time emotionally expressing myself in a *totally* different manner. This has to do with me exercising my creative energy. Most people will never really be able to tell the difference, but I can—and I can feel it even when other people are playing and expressing themselves differently.

To give you a visual, imagine playing a little minuet for an audience of old people that are dining. Now imagine playing the same minuet for a little 5-year-old girl that wants to dance next to your piano. The emotional expression in the two cases is radically different.

You *must* exercise your creative energy and emotional expression in as many ways as you can in every aspect of your life, or risk turning into a piece of cardboard that will attract nothing but roaches, because your system will not recycle, will not cleanse and will not rejuvenate itself unless you do so. I have encountered way too many women who are essentially dead inside despite eating properly, doing Yoga, working hard at their jobs and trying to be good moms, wives, partners, etc. simply because they don't express themselves creatively.

STOP MESSING WITH SUPERNATURAL TECHNOLOGY

I said earlier in this section that Hatha Yoga is not a workout. It is not exercise either, so what is it? Yoga, in all its forms, is an exceptionally powerful technology that will fundamentally alter and rewire your energy system. Hatha Yoga, while it may seem very easy and harmless on the surface, is a potent way of doing this that engages the physical body. In the hands of a true guru, Hatha Yoga can be used to transform an individual totally, changing everything about them including their looks, lifestyles, food preferences—everything.

And that is where the real problem lies, because a true guru will take responsibility for a disciple and direct every little aspect of their life, including what they eat, how they sleep, what they do, etc. In the hands of someone who isn't competent enough, Yoga is nothing short of a time bomb waiting to go off.

You may be lucky in that you're going to a studio that teaches you a few stretches and calls it Yoga, but if you hit the right pose in the wrong way, you can be sure the effects will ripple throughout your life. In the US, I've encountered many people who claim to be teaching Yoga and I know for a fact that either they are not teaching Yoga or they're basically orchestrating a disaster in slow motion for themselves and their students.

Ask yourself: does *anything* about Hatha Yoga look *natural* to you? In real life, when was the last time you needed to hit a pose like the ones you aim to perfect at your studio? However strange your local gym looks with all those weight plates and machines, lifting weights is something you do naturally, on a day-to-day basis without realizing it, while Hatha Yoga is a whole different beast. It is a supernatural technology. Don't mess with it.

If you want to fundamentally alter how you exist here on this Earth, then Yoga is for you. The practices I am describing in this book are essentially a form of Yoga, but one that relies on a higher intelligence coming into your system and leading you through it naturally, customizing it for you and only you. The practices in this book have to do with playing with water, eating, sleeping, exercising, getting in touch with the Earth, wearing sufficient clothing, living in discomfort, etc., all of which are ways to cleanse your system and invite a higher level of intelligence to come into your life. There isn't even a line on meditation techniques, because "meditation" is supernatural technology and one that I will never teach.

Just about any activity in the world can be turned into a form of Yoga, because Yoga has nothing to do with what you do and everything to do with the *way* you do it. The practices in this book, along with the narrative, will turn your existing lifestyle—whatever it looks like today—into Yoga, transforming you and your world in the process. This is the safest way to do it, but also why it is time limited. When the world changes, the practices, and the narrative, will need to change.

So, this is a warning to all of you Yoga fans who are taking things too lightly or are perhaps ignorant and don't realize what you are up to. If you want to practice Hatha Yoga, find a true guru and learn Hatha Yoga from them.

Or just go do simpler things like lift weights at a gym. You'll thank yourself later.

SLEEP

Probably the biggest lifestyle changes most of you will have to make to progress spiritually and become more intelligent lie in the areas of rest and sleep. If you found the sections on food and exercise difficult to accept, part of it may be because you currently don't have a supportive schedule of rest and sleep that makes eating well and working out hard possible.

REST

There is a big difference between resting and sleeping and at an energy level, they do totally different things. Your energy system is powered by you, not by the food you eat, and it is replenished only when you rest. Resting means that you are simply being—you are awake but not doing anything. You don't even need to close your eyes. When you don't rest enough, your energy system slowly starts to get depleted and over time, when it is low, you start suffering from a range of issues. Depression is a direct consequence of the lack of rest, and the only real fix is to rest until you've rested enough. But the more serious consequence of the lack of sufficient rest is that you become weak energetically and when that happens, your attention span suffers.

Over the last 42 years, I have never spoken to a woman that was able to focus on a topic for more than a few seconds at a time. Across the world, this is a problem that is widespread among women. This is not as true of men yet, but they too are slowly getting there. Women get distracted by something or the other every few seconds—usually their feelings, but also memories, ideas, or something that is happening in their environment around them. Many women have started lying to themselves that this is a consequence of the fact that they have many responsibilities, or worries and that they are juggling many things, but this is not the case. The real problem is that a weak energy layer causes the subconscious (which is chaotic in every one of your cases) to start popping up and interrupting your conscious experience every few seconds. What should be a silent ally becomes a problematic partner, constantly creating problems for you to solve, issues for you to pay attention to and things you must address.

When this happens, you become distracted by something or the other near *constantly* and you find yourself unable to hold a decent conversation, or if you do, find that you keep drifting from topic to topic without any coherence. This is not a state of normalcy, but a disease. And the only way to cure this disease is for you to rest, which means that you take time to simply *be*.

The practice in Chapter 9 is exactly what that is about—letting your system actually rest. Most of you will find that resting for 20 minutes at a stretch is a bit too much for you to handle, which is why it is the upper limit. Once you start to make some real progress though, you will naturally want to rest more, at which point, your practice will automatically evolve.

Rest at the physical layer does what most of you already know—it repairs whatever needs repairing, mostly. But if this is rest, what is the function of sleep?

SLEEP

Sleep is a totally different mechanism that *depletes* your energy reserves. Most people don't sleep for 8 hours a night or however many hours they are in bed, because a lot of that time is taken up in processing, which I don't count as part of sleeping. When your subconscious is processing and you're experiencing dreaming, you're still very much available to the body, so to speak. However, once your body decides it has processed enough, it decides to let you go—metaphorically speaking—and focuses entirely on its own growth. It is only that latter stage that I call sleep.

The *rest* component of sleeping is what repairs the body, but the *sleep* component, where you don't even dream, is what is used to *change* your life. Your body knows what tomorrow is going to bring, because it is in touch with the subconscious, and it uses sleep to literally prepare the body for what is to come. When you don't sleep well, your body is totally unprepared for the next day, spiritually, energetically, emotionally and physically. Instead of knowing how to handle life, it tries to figure out what to do as it's happening, which is not very efficient. In other words, your body struggles to *balance* itself as the day progresses and experiences unfold. What you experience when you don't have enough sleep is that nothing goes well, even if the world thinks it did.

When you've slept well, your body has basically figured out how to handle every incoming ball lobbed at you, how you are going to respond, how you are going to balance, what you need to eat, what you need to wear, where you need to go, etc. I mean this in a very literal sense—your life is planned out for you to the smallest detail, perfectly, when you are asleep. This is the whole point of sleeping—to prepare for what's about to happen.

I know from what I've observed on the streets of America that *none* of you sleep properly, not even one of you. Even the children are being deprived of sleep nowadays, because they never even finish processing the day. You already know exactly why this is—because you don't rest enough during the day!

In other words, if you don't rest enough, you won't be able to sleep! And here we are, in a civilization that believes they are the same thing.

HOW MUCH TO REST AND SLEEP

Together, you must have at least 12 hours a day of rest and sleep combined. I am basing this on what I've seen so far—for many of you the number would be greater. For a few of you, it would be smaller. However, in those 12 hours, you are allowed to dream as well. This means that if you are, in fact, practicing 20 minutes of silence a day, you'd be in bed for at least 11.5 hours every night. If this sounds impractical to you, it's only because you've pushed your system to the limit and are in dire need of so much sleep and rest.

My "sleep" component lasts about an hour a night. I don't need to sleep more, but in the colder months, I do enjoy dreaming, especially because my dreams tend to be about things that I pick up from people who live around me. My own processing is done by the time I go to bed, so I don't have dreams of my own, but our bodies are all transmitting and receiving constantly and when I am dreaming, I am usually receiving other people's transmissions and turning them into movies. It's as if I get to watch movies about what my neighbors are up to every night—and they are hilarious if you ask me, totally weird and useless. When your subconscious starts to quiet down, you too will start to differentiate between processing what has happened to you versus what you are picking up from the surrounding environment.

In your case, even though you are "asleep," you will end up spending a lot more time dreaming, processing, etc. (it doesn't matter that you don't remember your dreams), which means that you will give your system lots of time to quiet down, and then you may have a few minutes of sleep every night, typically towards the wee hours of the morning.

SLEEP ENVIRONMENT

Understand that your body is capable of happily sleeping in some of the worst environmental conditions possible. Things like rain and storms will not wake you up when you are settled and done processing. Do *not* arrange for your sleep environment to be totally dark and silent, because that is not the kind of environment we evolved in. If you've ever been to the woods at night, you'll notice it is quite noisy (often noisier at night than during the day!) and unless it is a cloudy, moonless, night, there's a fair bit of brightness as well.

It is best that you sleep on the ground, alone and totally naked. Do not cuddle up to someone else—it is a sick way of sleeping. Your body needs isolation to repair, rejuvenate and plan for tomorrow. At the end of the day, remember that experientially speaking, you have a life totally independent of everyone else, and sleep is your only chance to prepare for it. If you have young children and they want to cuddle up to you, fine—do not prevent them. But at least you and other adults must sleep without touching each other, in separate rooms if you have them, even if you're married.

If you want your body to be healthy and come back to normalcy, never sleep on a cushioned surface. The surface must be unyielding as much as possible. This means that you may sleep on a thin rug, thin carpet or the bare floor, but never a pad or a mattress. You may find this difficult if you are in a cold place, but you'll have to learn to get used to having at best a blanket underneath you and allowing your body to heat itself.

You are welcome to cover yourself with as many layers as you like, but in general, the fewer the better. If it's warm where you live, and you can sleep like a caveman—with nothing underneath, nothing on top and no clothes, you'll become totally immune to most diseases on the planet in about a year's time.

Use whatever pillow you want—it doesn't matter.

You must always have one or two elements in play around you (meaning in motion) when you sleep, because only when elements are in motion will they take away all the energetic trash (bad information) that you release at night. This means that you must either have a good breeze or a nice fan and/or a lamp (meaning fire, not electricity). In my home, I always sleep with at least one window open and a fan running at full speed, even though I am usually cold when I do that. Understand that fire is extremely energizing, and because sleep depletes your energy, a fire—even a tiny oil lamp—will keep you asleep a lot longer (a good thing), as long as it doesn't make you ungrounded and wake you up!

As much as possible, try not to sleep with only artificial air. In really dirty places like Los Angeles though, the pollution outside is often worse than indoors and you may be better off opening your windows only when it's raining and all the atmospheric filth is washed off.

I am sure you all know not to eat too close to bedtime. You must not feel full when you are in bed, but if you don't eat enough carbs, you will sleep poorly. The key is grounding—and you need some Earthy stuff before you go to bed, or you'll keep waking up at night.

It's a bad idea to have water, especially in a transparent container, sitting next to you when you're asleep. Sleeping involves cleansing and you don't really want anything around you that might pick up garbage which you then consume, once again.

The position you sleep in isn't that important. In fact, once you start sleeping on a hard surface, your body will naturally be very uncomfortable in the beginning and start to experiment with all kinds of things to make you comfortable. This, by itself, will cause you to start going to the gym or working out in some way. You won't even have to push yourself.

The truth about walking the path of light is that much of it relies on you being able to live in as natural a fashion as possible. Because I don't use any supernatural techniques such as meditation, tantras and such, you really will get the most out of your life by walking the path of light only if you live in an environment that allows you to live naturally, without too many support mechanisms. Naturally, if you live in a very cold place, a very windy place, a very rainy place or an excessively hot place, you are simply going to be unable to follow this path all the way. There is a very good reason why many yogis tend to gravitate towards places that are easier to live in naturally and this is true when it comes to sleep as well. No matter how much technology improves, there will never be a substitute for living in an environment that is naturally supportive to the human body.

PHYSICAL EXHAUSTION IS KEY

Part of the reason I've recommended a hard workout 6 days a week is because none of you are physically exhausted any more. Many of you are emotionally or psychologically stressed and *spiritually exhausted*, i.e., your energy layer is depleted, but physically, most of you have way too much energy at the end of the day. You should have trouble walking by the time you go to bed. At least, that's my standard—I can hardly pick myself up off the floor when it's bedtime. This means that you must *not* be spiritually exhausted during the day—something I'll talk about in the chapter on work.

If you don't have enough energy in your energy layer, you will not be allowed to sleep and your body will constantly wake you up, because it's only when you are awake that your energy layer is replenished with energy from you. This is partly what is being diagnosed as sleep apnea (not the obstructive kind), insomnia and so on. Fixing them is a simple matter of having enough spiritual energy and little physical energy when you go to sleep. When you work out hard, you will end up resting at some point during the day because your body will force you to, usually causing you to sleep better at night.

This goes without saying, but if you want a healthy lifestyle, including a good night's sleep, all caffeine, alcohol, drugs, stimulants, depressants, whatever—all must go. You won't be able to force yourself to let many of these go without causing some other problem in your system, and in the case of pharmaceuticals, you cannot let them go unless you are healed, so let the practices in this book take you there, particularly the one in Chapter 13. When you are healthy, you will sleep better.

NIGHTMARES

Many people think nightmares are a bad thing, but they are the best thing that can happen to you while you are cleansing on the spiritual path. Nightmares are a kind of *accelerated suffering*, the kind your subconscious can go through because it's not in the realm of time. A nightmare is your body's way of conjuring up all kinds of nonsense and putting you through it at a very quick pace to have you experience enormous amounts of pain and suffering in a very short amount of Time, releasing all that pain and suffering in the process. This means that whatever you would have experienced in real life over several weeks, you will experience in a few moments during a nightmare.

Remember that all experience starts from within and is then manifested in real life. Whatever "bad stuff" you experience in a nightmare is something you will *never* experience in real life, unless you keep repeating in real life whatever caused you to have a nightmare in the first place. What you face in a nightmare is basically checked off as "experienced," because during a nightmare you have no control, and therefore, you experience all the torture you have to as if you're absolutely helpless. As a result, Time moves forward quickly.

If you are a soldier, first responder or some other such professional, consider yourself lucky if you're having tons of nightmares. First, unless you keep living an idiotic life and subjecting yourself to bad experiences, those nightmares will come to an end at some point. Second, having nightmares means that you are *not* able to suppress the pain, which is a good thing. Instead of trying to force yourself into sleeping better, allow the nightmares to come and go. When they end, you will be better off, both in sleep and in real life.

FOOD, SLEEP, EXERCISE & DISEASE

The link between food, sleep, exercise and disease is very deep. Ultimately, all disease is a consequence of energetic imbalance, or invasion by a foreign body/organism. The latter isn't something you can do much about, other than living in a clean environment and perhaps taking a vaccine. However, nearly all other diseases that are being heavily treated nowadays with medication, surgery and such are simply due to energetic imbalances.

In fact, most of the diseases on the planet that are being experienced by people nowadays are a consequence of energetic *weakness*, which means that their inner, energetic layer is totally depleted. When this happens, your body creates and injects all kinds of chemicals into your system just to keep you alive, but if this situation continues, your body will die. Energetic depletion occurs mostly when people waste their energy on all kinds of frivolous and harmful activities, primarily for the sake of pleasure. Unlike happiness, bliss and ecstasy, which are powered by a deeper source, pleasure uses up your inner energy. When a human being engages in pleasurable activities, they keep depleting their energies and ultimately create a situation where the body can no longer survive. For such an individual, diseases are inevitable.

When I was working spiritually, I had many, many diseases, illnesses and ailments, not because I was experiencing pleasure but because I was literally giving my energy away to people who needed it. At some point during the first 33 years of my life, I was diagnosed with anxiety, sleep apnea, high blood pressure, pre-diabetes, eye weakness, arrhythmia, digestive issues, colon problems, bronchitis, asthma, demyelination of the nerves, food intolerances, environmental allergies and some other issues I can't even remember—and these are just the ones I was diagnosed with when I involuntarily ended up at some clinic or doctor's office. At one point, a neurologist told me I would end up with Multiple Sclerosis if I kept doing whatever I was doing. This was a ridiculous warning to me, because at the time, I was exercising regularly, eating very healthily and studying hard. I wasn't drinking, partying or even socializing too much—in other words there was absolutely nothing wrong with my lifestyle. I received many such ridiculous warnings and suggestions from many doctors during those years, none of whom had any idea why so much was going wrong in my body.

Once my healing period began, everything changed. I would often go to bed with severe symptoms relating to some disease or another and wake up totally free of them. This continued for months where illness after illness simply vanished, never to return. Today, my body experiences no illness whatsoever, save the occasional cough when the weather changes.

It is only because of my own life experience that I can say with total confidence that the modern medical system is a joke and one that is only good at one thing—providing short-term comfort. This short-term comfort comes at a high price—it can prevent healing *and* it severely depletes the energy reserves of the people who work in the healthcare industry, especially the ones that directly come in touch with patients. If you really want to heal and you have the energy needed to do so, you must cleanse energetically, do the practices in this book and live a clean life. This means you must eat well, work out hard, sleep well and do all the right things. Then suddenly, all those diseases that you were told you have because they are genetic, hereditary, environmental or whatever, will vanish over time. And of all the things that will help you get over your diseases and build strength, rest and sleep are #1. Make them a priority.

Understand that I am not the kind of yogi that is going to talk to you about faith-based healing, miracles or anything of that sort. All miraculous healing requires someone else to carry the burden you were supposed to carry and release you from the responsibility. I have no interest in people that refuse to carry their burdens themselves. If you don't have the energy to heal, the path of light will kill you. Take that into account.

A NOTE ON POISON

In the chapter on exercise, I said that working out really fast is a bad idea. The reason has to do with what happens when the body is suddenly shocked. When the physical body is suddenly shocked, it responds by flushing some of your bad information into the energy layer, because there is more stability to be found in the deeper layers of your body. Unfortunately, over time, all those imbalances will reappear in your system at some level—either your physical body will go back to being unbalanced or your life will become bad in some way. The short-term result though, is that your physical body will suddenly look better. This is what's going on with some of these violent mechanisms being used to fix the body's problems, like excessively intense workouts.

The same thing happens to your body when it is shocked in other ways, such as when you get overly drunk, go on a rollercoaster ride or constantly keep pushing the body too hard as many professional athletes do. In the case of things like alcohol, it poisons the physical body as well, causing it to get very sick.

The real benefit of this mechanism in the body is that you can use a *little* bit of a shock to get the body to become more alert and instead of pushing problems deeper, become aggressive at finding and kicking problems out. This happens when you have a little bit of poison, or when you have a little bit of fun, which are the same thing as far as the body is concerned.

When I say a little bit of poison, I am talking about, for example, getting jostled around a bit on the bus, riding a motorcycle down a bad road for a bit, jumping for a bit on a trampoline, getting bit by an ant, or having a swig of alcohol perhaps once a year or so, at best. The keyword is "a bit," i.e., not much and not regularly. A little bit of fun, aka poison, will improve your health and keep you free of disease. If you lived in a natural environment, you'd get enough of this daily to keep you super healthy.

ENJOY SLEEPING!

Sleep is a gift, and a need. Without sleep, existence is impossible. Our existence isn't made to remain in constant flow all the time. It is made like breath—expansion and contraction, filling and emptying. The same is true of our lives. You must empty yourself by giving all you have, and then take the time to rest and be refilled. If you don't do this, you'll simply die of fatigue and misery.

So, sleep all you want—don't listen to people who say you sleep too much. You would anyway be doing the planet a service by staying in bed instead of creating a mess outside. Plus, who knows—perhaps in your sleep you are laying the groundwork for a beautiful life in the future!

WORK

Possibly the most important thing that most people believe they do daily is work. Unfortunately, what most people consider "work" is totally useless and destructive, not just to the planet but also to their own lives. In this chapter, I will cover work, money and wealth to help you understand why we work, how those three things are connected and how you should be working in order to make the most of your time on this Earth.

WHY WORK?

The reason you work is not because you need to make money, as most of you believe, but because you have an innate need to work, thanks to the fact that you've not lived the way you needed to in the past. Inside every human being is a need for fulfillment, one that is naturally satisfied simply by being. Far from being something that a human being needs to seek, fulfillment is a natural condition of the human body, along with sweetness, happiness and satisfaction. As a child, you did not seek any of these things, nor did you ever have to. You simply woke up, played all day, got tired, ate and at some point, went to bed. Whatever cleansing was necessary happened along the way without you having to think about it or plan it in any way.

In other words, you were healthy.

As you grew older, at some point, the garbage of the environment in which you live started to grow beyond your ability to handle it, and so you needed to start doing things consciously to make sure that you could be clean. This process, where you feel like you must slog through something in order to get back to your natural state, is called "working." Unfortunately, at some point in history human beings forgot that work is supposed to be temporary—something you do as necessary and forget about as soon as it's over. This is directly connected to the development of civilization and the growth of the idea that pain and discomfort is a bad thing. As soon as human beings started to get comfortable, they lost their ability to cleanse themselves effortlessly, all the time. Suddenly, they found themselves unable to get through the day without having to work, because the natural feeling of fulfillment, happiness and satisfaction simply vanished. They had to work to find it again!

Once language entered the fray, human beings began to cook up stupid reasons for why they couldn't be happy and fulfilled unless something or the other on the *outside* was changed. This meant that human beings now needed to work even harder, both to change things on the outside, as well as to cleanse themselves, which only got harder the more the external environment got more comfortable.

Today, of course, civilization is at a peak and everyone who lives in a somewhat developed situation is quite comfortable. At this point, there is absolutely no way most human beings can stop working, even if they don't officially hold a job. They must work in some manner to constantly try and find that natural state once again, where they are fulfilled, happy and satisfied. It is for this reason that most human beings are relentlessly active—at least on the inside—and cannot be at peace anymore.

So, for all you young people who may be fantasizing about winning the lottery or having some situation come about that releases you from having to work, understand this much: you will only stop working when you are enlightened and not a moment sooner because enlightenment simply means you've come back to your natural state and are experiencing fulfillment, happiness and satisfaction without having to do anything. Until you reach that state, no matter how much money you have, things will constantly make you work in some fashion or another and there will be no escape.

Therefore, you might as well try and make work a productive, beautiful and useful experience instead of chasing a fantasy where you don't have to work.

The reason you should work as effectively as possible is so that you can bring work to a quick end. Yogis like me, for example, have worked whenever we have needed to with such ferocity, commitment and intensity, that most of the time we simply hang out or we enjoy whatever experience we are having in a state of total freedom and happiness. For instance, writing this book, while you may consider "work," isn't for me. I simply sit down when the mood arrives and the Divine Feminine takes over and starts typing while I enjoy the whole experience, which includes reading these words, sipping a cup of decaf, eating a slice of cake or whatever. I expend enormous amounts of energy while writing this book, but there is no feeling of working whatsoever. It's pure bliss.

This is where you need to get to—a state where living itself is enough, and whatever happens, happens without you having to work for it. In other words, activity takes care of itself while you sit back, relax and enjoy watching your body go through what it needs to go through, thank God! After all, at that point God is doing all the work, while you experience only bliss.

But why is work such a horrible experience? Let me help you understand what is going on using a simple example.

WHY WORK SUCKS

Say you are a barista at a coffee shop. Your "job," as defined by your employer, no doubt includes a range of activities, as well as the exercise of a bunch of "soft skills," as they say. You may need to make coffee, clean the counter and take out the trash sometimes, but you are probably also expected to smile, say hello, be polite, etc. If you are in a really demeaning environment, you may be required to actively try and please every customer. Why is that demeaning? Because you didn't come here to Earth to please anybody. But let's get back to your "job."

One fine day, while you are manning the front sales counter, a person comes in with a horrible attitude, bad energy and starts behaving obnoxiously. This person immediately starts to take advantage of your situation (you must serve them) and a horrible experience begins for you, where you have to more or less smile and pretend that everything is ok, while the person in front of you keeps making comments, insinuations, criticisms or perhaps is just behaving inappropriately. I know for a fact that people in the service industry are expected to deal with such situations and many of them do so daily. Women, especially, are constantly the target of idiots everywhere, because the service industry wants to advertise women and men as being "available" in some fashion and by nature, most women have no defenses in such situations (more on that in the chapter on feminine power).

Now the attitude of most people in situations like this is to try and ignore bad behavior, stuff down whatever they are feeling deeper and act like everything is ok. They may cry or take out their frustration and anger later, but most baristas continue to perform their "job" in the moment. If things get too difficult, they may put their foot down, "escalate" the situation by calling a manager, or the police in some cases. This is what most people are taught to do.

But why is such a thing even happening?

Once again, this is simply life trying to get rid of your garbage, your bad information. When you have issues inside, life will use *every opportunity* to give you a chance to face your problems and overcome them. This is life actively trying to help you get over your fears, doubts, uncertainties, false beliefs, insecurities, neuroses—you name it. If you haven't been cleansing on a regular basis, if you haven't been processing bad information in your dreams and nightmares and getting rid of them, you *will* have bad experiences in real life—there is nothing you can do about it. Even if the situation around you is pleasant, as long as your inner environment is a mess, you will basically be unable to handle whatever is going on and end up suffering in some fashion. Let me give you another example to help you understand what I am saying.

When I was in Los Angeles, I would often spend time at a particular coffee shop writing a blog for teenage girls. Often, homeless people would come by and start talking to me about various things, sometimes getting all worked up when I countered their confusion with wisdom. On one occasion, a homeless person became so upset at me that they started yelling, screaming and spitting at me. The staff at the coffee shop saw this and came out to help but the homeless person ran away. During that whole experience, I not only did not budge, but I smiled at everyone and continued with my work. Why? The homeless person's actions had nothing to do with me, and thanks to the fact that I wasn't confused about what I was saying or doing, I was happy no matter what was going on. In other words, the homeless person's behavior had no impact on me whatsoever. This wasn't true for me during my healing period, where the actions of people would upset me sometimes. The difference between the two states is that in the latter state, I had finished "working" on myself and had no problems to solve.

The reason your work and your work environment (and perhaps your whole world and your life) sucks is simply because your body is trying to get rid of trash. If you have issues, everything will suck. And since the feeling of work ends when you have no issues, this effectively means that work will always suck, until the end of all time.

In the past as well as today, people have tried all kinds of things to overcome this "problem" such as trying to create a better working environment with nice lighting and furniture, providing places to play, eat and do your laundry, even providing auxiliary benefits like vacation and childcare. And of course, there's always alcohol and marijuana, entertainment and escapist strategies galore. Nothing helps, because work will always suck. The only thing you can do is make sure you finish your work as quickly as possible and start living effortlessly. So, how do you do that?

SPIRITUAL PRACTICE AT WORK

Let's go back to the example of the barista. When you find yourself in a horrible situation, the most efficient thing you can do is to "take it," full on. Do not stuff your feelings deeper, do not pretend that everything is ok, do not smile if you are upset and do not force yourself to continue working as if nothing is wrong. You must *give in*, become totally vulnerable and allow whatever is bubbling up from inside to take over. If it makes you cry, fine. If it makes you scream, fine. If it makes you go crazy, fine. Don't misunderstand this to mean that you must "take out" your feelings on whatever is around you. Do not put on a show. You must experience it fully *on the inside*, but if the feeling causes you to involuntarily act in a certain way, fine. You must be totally honest with yourself and allow yourself to feel the full force of whatever is coming out of you, because what is going on is cleansing, not something bad in the world that you must fix or run away from.

You may have heard a piece of scripture somewhere that goes something like this: resist no evil. Well, this is what it means. You must not resist whatever it is that's going on. You must allow it to destroy you if it wishes. If *and only if* you can be this vulnerable in the world will you be able to continue walking the path of light. Any attempt to "show strength," "stand up for your rights," protest, complain, disrupt, fight or run will cause you to sink back into darkness. You must live on this Earth as if you have no rights, no guarantee of survival, no hope of rescue, no defenses and no recourse to justice. If the world around you wants to come to your aid, fine—do not resist that either. But *you* must never resist.

They say that the animalistic response in a human being is characterized by "fight or flight" behavior. Both the "fight" and the "flight" must leave you. And they will leave you when they have been beaten out of you. There is no other way.

You must give in and experience your inner turmoil no matter what, day in and day out, never ever trying to become invulnerable. When you do this all the time, you will become thinner and thinner, more and more vulnerable, until there is nothing left to protect you at all. You will have no smart retorts, nothing sassy to say, no threats to make, no barbs to trade and at the same time, you will stop looking for a way out. You will accept the simple fact that all that is going wrong in your world is simply due to your own body trying to cleanse itself. And once you truly accept that, you will shut up and take it.

I am not telling you that this is a state that you must live in temporarily, only to become a superhuman at some point and start beating the crap out of everyone that may have "wronged" you in the past. No, you must live in a state of utter defenseless vulnerability for the rest of your existence, because *that* is normal. And in that totally defenseless vulnerability lies the path to total freedom, bliss, fulfillment, happiness, satisfaction and the ability to invite love into your life. If this isn't hard enough, the path of light requires that you do this even if your life is in danger. Neither fight, nor flee, but accept whatever situation you are in, do what comes naturally, and shut up. It is this kind of vulnerability that myself and every yogi I have ever come across or even read about have lived with and continue to live with. When I warned you that survival is not guaranteed on the path of light, I meant it. Are you still interested?

Nearly 100% of you will fail this stage of the process, because you believe vulnerability is abnormal. The conditioning that most of you have been subjected to over millennia has taught all of you to either fight or flee (mostly fight at this point) and none of you believe that you must accept your fate and just be quiet. In fact, some of you are so allergic to the idea that you must be vulnerable, that when a man came and demonstrated this very principle, you concocted a bullshit narrative to explain away what He did. Yes, I am talking about Jesus.

Jesus didn't come to Earth to save anyone, nor has He saved anyone. He was sent here to demonstrate what happens when you speak the truth, walk the path of light and basically "shut up and take it." Sure, he took on some of the burdens of a few people, but that is something even I have done, as have millions of yogis before Him and since. It is this burden that causes people like us to be accused, persecuted, tortured in some manner, even killed, as Jesus was. It's life's way of cleansing what needs cleansing.

We no longer live in a world where you are likely to be publicly flogged and crucified simply for speaking the truth. However, if you walk the path of light, you *will* face all kinds of negativity in the world in which we live, and you will have to simply continue being silent and taking whatever treatment is doled out to you. My whole professional life working in the United States was *constantly* filled with negativity, with people accusing me of things I didn't do, saying things I didn't say, having attitudes I don't even understand or recognize. Consequently, I was penalized, punished, denied opportunities, whatever. Of course, I was never interested in worldly rewards, so those things never bothered me, but I had to endure the pain and suffering that comes with negativity, nonetheless.

If you want to succeed on the path of light, stop believing in bullshit narratives about saviourship, rescue and "forgiveness." These things are false and will make you fall off your path. Sure, there are many beautiful forces in existence that will help you (e.g., Grace, which I'll talk about later) but at the end of the day, you must experience what is yours to experience fully, not hope that someone will magically ensure that you can escape whatever it is you must face.

This is what it means to work. It has nothing to do with you being a barista, a police officer or an accountant. It has everything to do with whether you allow life to come in and take what it wants to take, leaving you bereft of what you had before so you can move forward with a little less baggage. You will not receive any special treatment from the universe because you "help people," "do good" or something of that kind. For instance, being a nice person, holding the door open for an old lady, helping the homeless, recycling, writing nice things in books—none of these things will get you any points. Whatever garbage you have inside, you must give up. And you give up your garbage by giving in to life.

EXCEPTIONS FOR WOMEN

There is only one thing that women are allowed to do that is different when it comes to bad situations: leave. Do not confuse this with "flight." The difference is that when someone is throwing trash at you, you need not stand there and take it. You can leave, but you will still have to experience whatever it is that's bubbling up on the inside, *in silence*. You still don't get to complain, protest, disrupt or whatever. You still don't get to try and "protect" yourself. But you are allowed to simply walk away, while a man must literally just stand there and take it.

The reasons for this are simple but profound and will only fully make sense once you read the chapter on feminine power, but the thing is, in existence, women are granted more freedom than men are. Additionally, no matter how far women go, the negative information that is thrown into them will be thrown into them even if they are not physically around. In other words, while men are expected to endure their pain *physically*, women are subjected to it *emotionally* and need not endure it physically as well.

And if you are a woman, when you decide to leave a bad situation, you are welcome to take your man, your children, your family—whoever it is you are leading—with you.

YOUR WORK ENVIRONMENT

The gist of the previous section is basically this: it makes absolutely no difference what you decide to do for work—*none whatsoever.* You are welcome to do whatever the hell you want. Almost 100% of our modern economy is based on creating comforts and pleasures while destroying the planet, so you will carry the burden of all that no matter what you do at work. There is no avoiding it.

So, can you simply decide to not work in our modern economy at all? Well, yes! If you decide that you don't want to work for the modern economy, you don't have to. You are welcome to find another way to survive if you like, but it's highly unlikely you will. In fact, simply spending time in silence as much as possible will result in you accomplishing a *lot* more work than you would by *going to work.* This is one reason why, whenever you see a powerful guru, you will often find a whole bunch of people simply sitting in silence in front of them. They are using the guru's energy and love to accomplish a boatload of work on the inside. They can make a tremendous amount of progress in this way and even go all the way to enlightenment simply by hanging out!

This is why the Divine Feminine has asked me to offer my home as a place to live and work for the young women of the world who wish to totally dedicate themselves to serving humanity. These women must work hard (not simply hang out), but at the same time, they will have more silence and a better environment to live and work in than anyone, anywhere. Simply spending time with me in silence accomplishes a lot of work.

Your ideal work environment should be completely silent, as much as possible. The sounds of nature are fine, but silence is even better. Work is a supernatural endeavor, one that animals don't do in the same way, for example. Their work is their life: eating, sleeping, procreating, etc. However, your work environment should be totally silent if possible because you need a whole different level of energy to support yourself. It is best if you work by yourself and not with other people, because contact with others will only *increase* the amount of work you have to do. You must always engage in activities that interest you and change your activities as necessary. Do not simply perform the same actions over and over like a robot if you don't care about them, because you will only regress by doing so. Even flipping burgers everyday can become yoga, meditation and a spiritual practice that enlightens, but you must be interested, engaged and focused. It is extremely important that women engage in creative work (and *only* creative work), as every other kind of work will simply deplete their energy and give them absolutely no benefits. Men, on the other hand, benefit greatly from having a physical component in their work, in some way. Depending on how you are made, you may find a mix of these two to be best for you.

It's important that you work no more than 4 hours a day. When I say that, I mean 4 hours of *focused, creative work*. Most of you engage in less than 15 minutes of actual work in a day, so do not think that you are all working too much. Most of you are simply doing the wrong thing in the wrong way, which is why you are exhausted spiritually, have trouble sleeping, seeing life clearly and so on.

That's all there is to it. If you simply accept life as it comes, you will naturally end up in the best place for you to work and grow, because all the other factors that make a workplace environment good have nothing to do with the work itself and have everything to do with what your body wants—fresh air, sunshine, good food, time for rest, a clean environment, etc.

By the way, all this brings to the fore the question: why are people so exhausted? What does it mean to do the wrong thing in the wrong way?

HOW WEALTH WORKS

A very long time ago, when slavery was common, the Egyptians employed thousands, if not hundreds of thousands of slaves to build great monuments that we today call the Pyramids. These monuments were built not just by the power of the Sun, but also by the energy of human beings. Human beings *literally* poured their own life energies into the work they did daily to create these massive structures. There was no small amount of creative power involved as well, something that is usually not acknowledged in popular narratives.

At the time, slaves were not given anything as a form of payment. They were simply fed, clothed and sheltered minimally. Slavery is basically a very direct way of exhausting a human being's (or another creature's) life energy to create something in the world. Slavery means that the life energy of a human being is transformed into whatever is being created, destroying the existence of the human being in the process.

Over time, this became untenable, not because people started to resist slavery, as is popularly believed, but because human beings simply started to run out of energy. It is not that human beings are *inherently* lower on energy today than in the time of the Pharaohs, but the availability of energy among human beings has fallen drastically thanks to the prevalence of bad information that blocks human beings from accessing their energy. Most of you who are depressed, for example, are not out of energy, but are unable to access it because there are issues in your energy system that keep you from being able to do so. As the amount of energy available among human beings started to fall, we had to come up with ways of accomplishing things that didn't require as much human energy.

Enter machines, which harnessed the power of the Sun (directly or indirectly through fossil fuels) to aid that part of human endeavor that was primarily mechanical in nature. In other words, everything needed to create something, except creative power itself, was now available in a manner that didn't require human intervention. But this created a problem: people who had wealth before thanks to many slaves who created wealth for them by constructing monuments, mining for gold, etc. now no longer could engage in the same kinds of activities simply by using machines. Wealth creation still needed creative power.

This is the case because in our world, wealth isn't about simply "owning" a piece of land or having access to a resource. For example, if you owned 100 acres of land, you may be considered wealthy on paper, but at the end of the day, it's useless unless it makes your life better. Even today, there are many vast tracts of land in the American Southwest that one can own but are quite useless because you cannot do much with them. Wealth isn't about simply having something in your name, but the ability to engage in activity or accomplish something, which requires more than just access to a resource. It also requires that you be able to make use of that resource in some way. It requires creative power.

This creative power comes only from human beings, especially human beings blessed with an elevated level of femininity, because creativity is primarily a feminine trait.

So, what happened in our world is this: the few that used to harness thousands of slaves, and their creative power, now needed a different way of harnessing human creativity while at the same time ensuring that those who gave up their creative power did not receive in return wealth commensurate with what they were giving up. For a few to have a lot of wealth, it is extremely important that they be able to harness the creative power of many without giving much in return. And this needed to happen without engaging the masses in physically taxing work.

Enter the "knowledge economy," a system where many engage in activities that aren't at all physical in nature but require giving up a huge amount of creative power, while a few can make use of that creative power in order to create wealth for themselves. In the case of the slaves that built the pyramids, every single slave contributed at least a little bit of intelligence and energy to the monuments they built. The Pyramids could never have been built by an army of cows, for example, no matter how much "direction" they are given. Nowadays, this intelligence and energy combined (aka creative power), comes from millions and millions of people, all of whom contribute towards the creation of monuments, except these monuments are no longer in the form of Pyramids. They are in the form of buildings, cars, yachts, and most importantly, money.

HOW MONEY WORKS

It used to be that money represented material wealth. Coins used to be made of precious metals and were by themselves valuable. Rulers of all kinds kept storehouses of gold, silver and other such resources, because that's how wealth was represented in the past. However, holding wealth in this way became simply impractical, as it is cumbersome to have to use material objects to trade. Enter currency, which makes all of it easy and painless. Having started out in material form, now currency is invisible, especially with things like crypto.

But something else changed along the way as well. Money became totally disconnected from the notion of actual wealth. Now, the value of money itself fluctuates daily, meaning that all the money in the world can become useless in the blink of an eye, depending on what the world economy is doing. Money is no longer real, but in fact, just a shared belief.

Unfortunately, most people haven't realized that this has happened, at least not to the extent that they should. People have continued to go to work, contributing their precious energies to whatever is asked of them. They have continued to give up their creative power to create wealth for the global economy. But instead of receiving wealth in return (at least slaves used to be fed, clothed and housed), now all people receive is a token that, at best, can be exchanged for actual wealth. In other words, human beings, who used to receive very little in return for their contributions, now receive nothing more than a *promise* of wealth.

If the money that people received was commensurate with what they gave up, and people were, in fact, able to exchange money for actual wealth, there would be absolutely no problem in the world. But this is not possible, because creative power is *real*, limited and *impossible* to represent in money terms. No matter how much money you receive, it will not be enough because *the creative power you gave up is what you need to create a beautiful life for yourself.* In other words, when you go to work, you give up what is basically your most precious resource and receive in return a pittance, which is why it is aptly called "compensation." Even the word itself clearly conveys that you're being given something that cannot make up for what you've given up. And this is why you're all exhausted at the end of the day, while accomplishing nothing of value for yourselves.

So, working for money is useless, unless you can find *other* human beings to give up *their* creative power in return for that money so you can have actual wealth. This is what we call "buying" things—we exchange money for something that is real. But when you do that, you too, give someone far *less* than what they had to give up creating that same artifact. Don't be confused about this—no matter how expensive you think something is, more was spent by people who created that thing than they will ever be compensated for. This is one of the reasons I always tip very well, because I know for a fact that the people who perform certain kinds of services (e.g., cooking in a restaurant) are giving up a lot more energy than they can ever be fairly compensated for.

THE CONSEQUENCE

The sum total of all these "developments," is that we have created a system that relies entirely on exploitation to keep the world running. At every stage in our global economy, human beings who give up their creative power get poorer, while human beings that use others' creative power get richer. What does this mean for you? It means simply this: if you want to be wealthy, you *must* exploit people, directly or indirectly. And if you *are*, in fact, wealthy, you *have* been actively exploiting people, directly or indirectly. There are no two ways about it.

This phenomenon of exploitation isn't new, of course. It has been going on for millennia now. But what's changed is that the system of exploitation has become invisible, hidden from view, and at the same time, acceptable. Even ordinary human beings are now trying their level best to get as many other human beings as possible to pay attention to them, to give them their creative power, their time, their energy, their attention—anything at all—so they can try to convert it into wealth for themselves. You may have heard of some of these people—the so-called "influencers," "celebrities," "media personalities" and such--who are nothing more than circus acts attempting to fleece people into giving up whatever energy they have so they can use it instead.

Understand this clearly: it doesn't matter how "indirectly" you may be exploiting people—the burden of exploitation is yours to carry. This is why the wealthy have absolutely *no chance* of ever completing their spiritual journey, finding truth, beauty and love, living a beautiful life or doing anything good for the world. And this applies to just about everyone that is trying to draw attention to themselves to become wealthier, more influential, more powerful, whatever.

So, if you don't want to be part of this system, what do you do?

HOW TO WORK WELL

No, you don't have to quit your job, start a hippie commune and rail against the system. Your predecessors tried that and failed for a good reason. The reason being that *work is important*. If you don't work, your life will be at a standstill. You must work, but you must do it differently. What does that look like? Let's get back to the coffee shop.

If you are a barista, what you must do is stop paying attention to what you are doing and start paying attention to the *way* you are doing it. This will be difficult for you in the beginning, because you don't even know what I am talking about when I say *the way*. The way you are doing something isn't an attitude, but an actual shift in focus and attention. All I can tell you for now, is that it will come to you, if you keep pondering over all you have read so far, practicing what I've laid out and letting your subconscious figure it out, because it takes a level of clarity for you to start seeing *the way* you must do something. When this begins to happen, you'll find that you care less about exactly what you are doing (say, making coffee) and start caring about *why you are doing it the way you are doing it* at that moment. Instead of being bored with your job, however mundane it might be, you will suddenly become extremely interested in every little detail of your work, no matter what you do. For example, your body will start to experiment with different ways of making coffee *on the inside*. This means that while you may seem to be making coffee using the same steps on the outside, *on the inside*, your energy, focus and attention will be on different aspects of the coffee making process, every time. I am not talking about your feelings; you will literally start seeing the *process* of coffee making in a different way every time you do it. Literally every single cup of coffee you make will be an entirely different thing, because it is, in fact, an entirely different thing. This may result in you changing the way you make coffee on the outside as well, i.e., you may do steps in a different order, skip steps because you found an easier route, etc. You will start to do everything you do this way, paying very close attention to every little detail, as if you are trying to peel a layer off the world and trying to peer inside. You may even start to see your whole job as a sacred task.

What will happen is that your body will start to accept that the world as you see it is just an illusion, that there is a world of energy underneath, and it will start to come in touch with that world bit by bit. For you, this process will be subconscious. Only if you live with me will I raise your energy to the point where this becomes conscious for you, because coming into touch with the reality of the world suddenly is disturbing and frightening, to say the least. The level of corruption, decrepitude, loneliness, sadness and perversion in our world is so great that if you came in touch with it unprepared, you'd die of heartbreak.

If you keep progressing this way, there will be times in your life where things will suddenly become no longer interesting. When this happens, it means your body has finished with what it was trying to figure out using the experiences you were having so far. In work terms, this will usually mean that you'll make a change in your career, the place you work, the responsibilities you take on, or something else. Basically, your life will change because your body wants a different set of experiences to keep moving forward. And when it does choose a new job, it will not care much (or at all) about the salary, benefits or any of those things that others care about. You'll simply care about whether you are able to continue paying attention to what you care about, understanding life and moving forward. You will be interested in life, not the world.

As your body grows in understanding, intelligence, clarity and power (the latter is what allows you to pay attention for longer periods of time without interruption), its energies will start to come under its own control. Once this happens, it's all over—you will no longer give up your creative power to benefit someone else. This means that you will spend 100% of your time, attention, energy, resources, indeed everything you have, on doing only what you care about.

At that point, instead of being a part of the system and being used as a slave to support it, you will be outside the system, *while still using the system to your benefit*. You will start to squeeze the system for good, instead of it squeezing you. You won't even know you're doing this, but you will do it, and it is what the world needs. Let me give you a simple example from my life.

In order to write this book, I am using a laptop computer that I bought from an online store and my phone's WiFi hotspot. There are many corporations involved in serving me, but I give them *only money*. I spend no time, attention, energy or personal resources on them whatsoever. When I shop, it takes me less than a minute to find and order what I need. I am never distracted, I never click on ads, read any of the messages that companies send me, and I don't provide feedback on surveys even when asked in person. Basically, I couldn't care less if the companies that serve me even existed. It makes no difference to me if this cell phone dies because I'll replace it without even blinking—and I won't give a damn what my body chooses. The money that I have was given to me when I was working in corporations and universities in America, but while I was working for them, despite fulfilling my responsibilities, I gave them nothing in terms of my energy—I was focused entirely on my spiritual work and the rest took care of itself. All the energy I used for my worldly work I picked up from other people and the environment I was in. I didn't expend a single ounce of my own energy to move the world forward, using it instead only to uplift and enlighten human beings. In other words, the system has been feeding me all these years and I haven't spent an ounce of energy actually contributing anything back to it. This is why, even at 42 years old, I have more energy than most teenagers do.

The flip side is that I never cared about money, promotions, accolades, reputation, influence or anything of the sort. As a result, I live in relative poverty for someone with my talents and capabilities, eat simple food, sleep on the floor, etc. But this is the life I was asked to lead, and I am very fulfilled, happy and satisfied. In fact, I am ecstatic, all the time!

This is how your life will evolve when you start to work well, care about *the way*, and forget about *the what*.

If you want to walk the path of light, you *must* embrace a life of minimalism, a life of poverty, a life of living on as little as possible, just enough for you to do the work you came here to do, to accomplish whatever you came here to accomplish, to live the beautiful life you came here to live, and no more. This does not mean that you must become homeless, turn into a hippie or somehow become a burden on everyone else. But it does mean letting go of everything that life takes away from you, with no thought of replacing it unless life itself brings it back to you.

And whatever you don't hold on to will be taken from you, guaranteed.

Once you start paying attention to *the way*, your co-workers will never see you the same way again. Your boss, your friends, your family, even people you randomly meet will start to avoid you, because they don't want what you are offering: freedom. You will find yourself isolated, maybe even ostracized, and having to live alone. Unless you have a partner who is very committed to walking the path of light, you will not find others to really connect with, because they simply won't understand why you are not interested in the world and all its toys. Entertainment, social media and all the ways in which you were engaged in the world will disappear over time, never to reappear. You will live in the *real world*, the world of sunshine, rain and butterflies—the world I live in. And you have absolutely no idea just how beautiful your real world will become—you will have to arrive there to believe your eyes. It will actually *look* different in a way I cannot explain to you.

COMMITMENT, REDUX

People like me, Jesus or the many saints and sages that have come and gone all embraced a life of poverty because we reject the world and its machinations. We reject exploitation in all its forms, visible and invisible. We reject the system totally, while still using all that is in civilization to carry out the work we must do unabashedly, knowing that at the end of the day, we give far, *far* more in real terms than what we ever receive from the world.

It is not possible to make the world a better place, but it is possible to replace it with reality, a better world. If you want to live a beautiful life and create a better world, you must be willing to use the world as it is and everything in it without resorting to judgment, while at the same time not becoming addicted to any of it. No matter how you live, most human beings on this Earth will find your lifestyle difficult to understand, reason about, put into words and justify. Only *you* will understand how you live as you progress, which is why you must never criticize the way someone else lives their life, even when you recognize that their way is harmful to you. Just keep your distance from anyone that isn't good for you, that's all.

Unless you are prepared to live this way, throw away this book, and consider yourself a failed candidate, because if you cannot commit to living up to a much higher standard than you ever knew was possible, and do that in the face of obstacles, challenges, persecution, poverty, even the threat of dismemberment and death, you will not succeed. The universe isn't handing out participation medals.

Why do I keep discouraging you from following the path of light? Because if you start, you *must* finish, or it's better you don't start at all. Going halfway and stopping is *very* painful because you will have neither meaning in your life, nor will you be able to place a blindfold over your eyes and enjoy the world like most people do. I don't want you to think that this is something you can try, put aside at some point and go back to what you were doing before, because you won't be able to.

This is a one-way path. The point at which you begin, is the point of no return.

FEMININE POWER

The result of all the practices in this book is that you will awaken the feminine within you, regardless of your gender. Awakening the feminine within is what actually turns the boys into men and girls into women. Awakening the feminine is what growing up is all about, not holding a job, paying taxes and having a home. Awakening the feminine is what most of the world's population has failed to do for as long as humanity has been around, and this failure is the reason our world is in such bad shape. But what is the feminine?

THE FEMININE

Most people, when they think of "the feminine," think of women, or they have some strange idea of what it means to be feminine. Many women equate femininity with being "girly," adopting a set of behaviors, activities or a way of dressing. But femininity has nothing to do with appearances. It is a primordial element, one that actually is responsible for the creation of all that is.

The feminine is the dynamic principle of the universe and exists as a counterpart to the masculine principle. While the masculine is empty like the sky, featureless, stable and unmoving, the feminine is dynamic, varied and beautiful. It is because there is such a thing as the feminine that there is creation and why it is in constant motion. The feminine is life-giving, life-sustaining and in fact, life itself. Everything that you can see, taste, touch, smell and hear is *essentially* feminine in nature, while the masculine provides the background against which all motion and dynamicity can be perceived. To put it simply, the masculine provides the background and the feminine provides the foreground. It is for this reason that yogis in the past have described life as a kind of game, or play, because at the end of the day, when you strip away all the narratives, the falsehoods and limited perceptions, all you see is the feminine dancing against a backdrop that is unmoving, like a ballet dancer on a dark stage.

Ultimately, femininity is a kind of intelligence, not some kind of "trait." You *can*, as most people are doing, ignore the feminine and destroy all there is in hopes of imposing order, consistency and constancy on creation. But if you want to live here harmoniously, joyfully and really dance your way to your destination, you must develop feminine intelligence, which encourages adaptation, evolution and most importantly, *inconsistency*.

INCONSISTENCY

If you take a close look at your life on a day-to-day basis, you will see that it is, in fact, totally inconsistent. You don't actually get up at the same time every day, or even breathe the same way from one moment to another. There are cycles, even in nature, but those cycles are very rough and not something you can set your clock to. You can spend all day at the ocean and not see the same wave twice. And if your perception is clear enough, you'll see that people are constantly changing. Absolutely nothing stays the same from one moment to another, and neither must your existence.

This whole idea that things should be predictable is a disease, one carried by people that don't have the energy or the intelligence to move, flex and flow with life. In the world of such people, every little change requires management of some sort. Essentially, people who like consistency live like cinder blocks, meaning that they refuse to adapt, shift and change naturally. Instead of embracing subtlety, which is what the rest of life is trying to do, they try to accumulate as much as they can and become bigger cinder blocks. But cinder blocks, due to their heaviness and their shape, cannot respond to a gentle breeze or even a river—they need a raging torrent, a flood or some other disaster that will cause them to move.

That is what we're seeing the Earth provide with increasing frequency—not just natural disasters, but societal upheavals, disruptions, protests, conflicts and conflagrations. One way or another, those who refuse to embrace inconsistency will be worn down, so you don't have to worry about them. All you must do is make sure that you are intelligent enough, and *sensitive* enough, that when the wind starts to blow in a different direction, you know what to do.

This takes a lot of practice, because at this point, all of you are heavily conditioned to value consistency, right from childhood. Even your idea of adaptation and evolution involves changing in a way such that you can ensure a consistent result at the end. Some of you may be thinking that I am talking about "going with the flow," or "living in the moment," but I am not. First of all, on this Earth there are billions of "flows," and you don't know which one to plunge into. Second of all, everyone already lives in the moment—you don't actually have a choice in that matter—but the problem is that the moment is full of all kinds of stuff, and you don't know what to pay attention to. So how do you practice inconsistency, identifying the "current of life" and paying attention to it?

Once again, this requires that you minimize bad information in your system, because that's what's keeping you from doing all those things. But as far as inconsistency goes, there is something very simple you can do to develop it.

"TIMELESS" DAYS

As often as you like, but preferably one day a week, live without any sense of time, measurement, information or anything that gives you a point of reference about the world in which you live. This means that on that day, you don't pay attention to your watch or clock, you don't read the news, you don't watch TV or social media, you don't engage in activities that require you to reason in any way and you certainly don't go anywhere you could be exposed to more information.

You can take this practice as far as you like, but the less contact you have with symbolic information, the better the day will turn out for you. You are welcome to turn off your phone and all electronic devices, turn off all your clocks, even turn off the electricity if you really want to go far (I wouldn't advise it). You can stay home unless you have a means of transportation that is "manual" (like a bicycle) to a place where there is nothing but nature and spend time there all day. You can make this fun if you like by camping on your porch all day, although if this means buying more stuff, it's counterproductive. And you would eat food that is basic, not something that requires elaborate means of preparation involving measuring, timing, etc.

On this day, you make no plans whatsoever and you do whatever the hell you feel like doing, although most of you will find yourself severely handicapped by the lack of an electronic device, a book, a puzzle, or something to occupy yourself with because almost everything people do nowadays involves using symbolic information. You will obviously not be able to talk to anyone but whoever's around, but beware—as soon as you start talking, you are likely to establish a point of reference of some sort, which is exactly what you don't want on this day. The point of this exercise is to force yourself to pay attention to life itself and not to anything in particular.

If you are smart, you will simply rest all day, which is the point of having all this time off on the weekends from work. You may discover there are things you can do to be active and engaged without using symbolic information, such as making music, dancing, painting, singing, etc. You will be forced to organize your life such that before this "Timeless" day comes around, you've already finished all your chores and organized things such that you don't have to go fiddling around for things you need, like laundry.

I can guarantee you that doing this properly for even one single day will change your whole outlook on life. Things will happen to you that you didn't expect, questions will come up that you never thought you had, life will start to reveal itself to you in ways you didn't think you would ever see, and *profoundness* will enter your life. In other words, you will start to see that your life has meaning without the need for any kind of belief system. Keep up the practice regularly, and your whole life will become "Timeless" at some point.

This is how my life is, every day—and it has been all my life. Yes, I've had clocks and a phone, etc., but those numbers don't mean a thing to me, because I simply don't go by time. I am not interested in knowing if something (like a store) is open, because I tend to go there and find out in person. I don't ever talk to people about mundane nonsense. Even when they're talking about sports or cooking, I am always sharing insights about life. I don't have a schedule, I don't eat the same thing every day, or in the same way and I work as and when I must. In other words, the only point of reference in my life is me!

So how did I make this work all those years when I had to go to the office? Simply by being available all the time and letting the world tell me where I had to go, what I had to do, etc. I would naturally get up early in the morning and go to work, usually before anyone else got there and just hang out. I mean it—sometimes I would sit in the sun for an hour before any of my coworkers showed up. When they needed a meeting, I said OK and set it up on the spot. When I had a task to do, I simply did it instead of putting it off for later (in my life, there *was* no "later"). I literally did everything as soon as I had to do it. If I got tired, I stopped and then started when I had energy again. When I was hungry, I rounded up whoever was interested in going to lunch and just went. In my experience, there was no planning, no estimation, no analysis and no reporting, even though my job involved planning, estimation, analysis and reporting! I just did things as I went along, without ever thinking about any of it.

You might think this is weird, but sometimes I used to accomplish more work in 15 minutes than most of my coworkers did in weeks. Of course, at every job, eventually there came a point where people decided that all the analysis and reporting was more important than actual work, at which point I simply left and allowed life to give me something else to do, if it cared to do so. This means that I've spent periods in my life doing nothing—and you must be willing to live like that too.

EFFORTLESSNESS

The key to living intelligently is to not make any effort. Just don't bother making an effort at accomplishing a goal, because if you are living the life you set out to live, what you came here to experience will come to you without you having to ask for it. All that effort that so many of you are putting into things is literally wasted energy because effort does not make *an iota* of difference in terms of how life actually goes. The reason all of you have an experience of effort is simply because you have all this bad information inside you that causes your system to act like a cinder block, resisting every single thing life is giving you at every turn. Once you start living "Timelessly," stop making an effort and rely only on *yourself* to decide where to go and what to do, you will effortlessly find the current of life that will guide you the rest of the way.

Understand that relying on yourself does not mean relying on your feelings, which is unfortunately what so many are trying to do. If you rely on feelings, you will do whatever the world wants you to do, not what you came here to do. Your feelings and thoughts are basically the garbage of the world circulating in your system. They cannot and should not be relied upon in any way. Relying on yourself literally means that you hang out until you have clarity on what to do next, do it and then go back to rest. That's all.

It is such a simple thing—waiting for clarity to arrive before you act—but it has become such a big problem that entire religions have been invented to give people guidance on what to do with themselves. All kinds of narratives have been foisted upon human beings over millennia as to who is out there directing all of creation, what they want from you, what the purpose of your life is and why you must do *this* and not do *that*. All of it is bunk.

There is absolutely *no one* out there directing your life and no one waiting for you to die. There is absolutely no plan for your life. You are in charge, but only to the extent that you can pay attention a certain way, and you must live your life intelligently, responding dynamically as life moves. Instead of giving yourself over to other people (e.g., your teachers, parents, boss, advertisers, etc.) and allowing them to guide you, you simply need to come back to your natural state, where you wait for clarity to arrive before you make a move. It is only when you practice waiting for clarity will you really experience it for yourself. And as you practice, you will gain confidence that in fact, clarity *will* arrive at some point and that you must simply wait in the best shape you can.

This confidence, that clarity will arrive at some point, is faith.

FAITH

Faith isn't some kind of belief that something you "want" will happen, or that a "God" will come down and take care of things and make things alright, etc. Faith is simply waiting for clarity, acting on it, learning from it and trying again. As I've shared with you throughout this book, this does not mean an escape from pain, an end to discomfort, the guarantee of material prosperity, the certainty that you will "win" at something, or even survival. It just means that your life will go well, i.e., it will go in the right direction, the direction where you will become wiser, more intelligent and closer to the possibility of being able to invite love into your life.

But what does all this have to do with the feminine anyway? Simply this: awakening the feminine fills your life with a power that allows the highest level of intelligence to enter. This power, which is essentially femininity itself, is what allows any of us to live a life without encountering too many obstacles. In fact, it is so synonymous with femininity that many girls are named after it: Grace.

GRACE

Of all the things that I've heard people speak about, Grace is one of the most misunderstood. I've heard people describe Grace as some kind of magical power that wipes clean all that a human being may have done wrong and still allows them to ascend to Heaven, or some other similar kind of nonsense. It is nothing of the sort. Grace is a power, *the* feminine power, that creates space for *love* to enter. Since love is the highest form of intelligence there is, when someone operates with Grace in their life, it means that love is functioning on their behalf, directing their life in a way that is beyond the capability of anything else. Far from overcoming obstacles, Grace ensures that you don't encounter them.

Unfortunately, Grace isn't something that is given to you "for free," in the sense that you cannot simply expect Grace to be in your life unless you do the necessary spiritual work. This is the greatest misunderstanding people have developed thanks to some scripture or another that apparently makes such a claim. Grace is something that is given to you when you accept your life as it comes and don't resist it. The reason that people have misunderstood this concept is simple: it is given to *whomever* accepts life as it comes. Let me give you an example.

Let us say that you work in the pornographic industry as a female performer. Your life is generally a horrible experience (even if you don't realize it), because it involves the world squeezing the life out of you in order to amuse and please whoever is interested. As a human being, most likely you are looked down upon by most people in society even though they may be benefiting or taking advantage of your situation in some way. Perhaps one fine day you decide to practice "Timelessness" and come to the realization that your life is more important than you thought it was and that you don't want to give it away to people who don't love you. You decide to make a change and quit the industry.

If you are honest with yourself, you will go through a long period of feeling like garbage, as all the trash that you accumulated while you were performing, both from people who were performing with you, as well as people who were enjoying your performances, starts to leave you. You will have to contend with all kinds of negative attention and perhaps find yourself in a place where you cannot make friends, because almost everyone you knew was in the world you are trying to leave behind. If you are honest with the world, you would tell them the truth about who you were and what you did prior, which would get you into lots of trouble, or at the very least, cause you to not be seen as desirable by some. But if you want to walk the path of light, you will have to live in an utterly defenseless and vulnerable manner, which isn't going to be easy at all.

In other words, you will have a hell of a time in this world, one way or another. But *only* if you accept your life as it unfolds, don't complain, don't try to hide, don't try to manipulate people in any way and suffer the consequences of your past life, will Grace come into your life. But the good news is, if you *do* live a life like that, Grace *will* come into your life. That's the promise.

Remember I said to you that walking the path of light is walking through the desert to a bus stop? The ride is free, but only if you are willing to throw away all your baggage, all your protection, all your masks and get on the bus naked, so to speak. Unfortunately, almost everyone I've spoken to believes that Grace is yours even if you get on the bus with all your baggage. It doesn't work like that—you won't even be allowed onto the bus!

By the way, Jesus demonstrated exactly what happens when you don't have Grace in your life. He was denied Grace for a reason, and He had to suffer enormously before He was finally allowed onto the bus. This happened to me for 26 years of my life.

Starting from when I was around 7 years old, until I was done with my spiritual service, Grace was withheld from me. I kept serving, working as I needed to, but literally *everything* would go wrong in my life in some fashion or another. Every flight I would get on would be delayed, applications would be rejected for stupid reasons, people would get upset at me randomly, and I would get cheated, robbed, beaten—you name it. When I first arrived in the US, even though I was legal, it took me 6 years to manage to get a driver's license because of some small issue or another with my documentation. And the whole time, the people in my life were constantly negative, either interfering with my way of life, criticizing me for what I did (or didn't do), even coming up with explanations to say that I was mentally ill, emotionally disturbed and so on. Even total strangers would behave inappropriately with me wherever I went. And thanks to being in surrender, I had no option but to tolerate it all as best as I could.

To be honest, my *real life*, even during those times, was spectacularly beautiful and on the *inside*, I was at peace, but in the *world*, all I did was suffer.

As soon as Grace entered my life, it *literally* became easier, and easier and easier, a process that continues to this day. Yes, even after Grace entered my life I had to deal with setbacks, but the difference was that post-Grace, all my so-called difficult experiences served only to *unburden me*, while pre-Grace, every difficult experience piled on more burdens and more problems for me to solve.

Nowadays, it is not uncommon for me to simply walk into an ordinary cafe, for example, and be *proactively* greeted, guided and assisted with finding something to eat and drink, finding a place to plug in my laptop and so on even though none of them have met me before. People often solve problems before I have them. That's what Grace does—it makes life easier, no matter how complicated the world becomes. Yes, it is a supernatural force—you'll have to experience it to believe it.

Awakening the feminine means to invite Grace into your life, or in the case of women, to awaken the Grace within, because women are naturally gifted with this power that they simply fail to develop.

BEING A WOMAN

The young women of today have absolutely *no clue* who they are, why they are here and what they came here to do. Among the thousands of young women I have encountered during my life and especially during my travels around the United States, I can tell you that I have met *not even one* woman who knows who she really is. Far from being carriers of Grace, storehouses of wisdom and leaders of the world, women have been forgotten and instead replaced with caricatures that serve either as props, toys or something worse.

This is true even of the women that the world generally considers "successful," because even *they* are operating at a very low level of intelligence and power compared to what they are capable of. It is not surprising to me that most people no longer genuinely respect women, because underneath all the narratives about empowerment and progress, the truth of the plight of women is known to all subconsciously.

And the truth is this: they are an upgrade over the male, far more intelligent, far more powerful and far more creative! I am not sure where all these idiotic narratives about women being somehow *less* than men started, but the truth is that women are *farther along* spiritually than men ever will be, at least when it comes to their potential. Women are innately blessed with so much more than men are that I could write many volumes on the subject, but I have been asked not to. Why?

The Divine Feminine wants to give women *one last chance* to discover and prove themselves, not to the world or to the universe, but to themselves. She wishes that women take the lead on their own spiritual development, enlighten themselves and share with the whole world what it's like to be a woman who truly sees all. Unlike the boys, each woman is *utterly unique*—a trait that comes with femininity and one that men gain when they awaken the feminine within themselves. Each woman is like a planet unto herself. Women are not from Venus, but a woman can be Venus, while another woman is Earth, another Mars and so on. The Divine Feminine wants women to have one last chance to show the world how incredibly unique and beautiful each enlightened woman's perspective on life can be and by doing so, inspire young women to take the lead in every aspect of society.

If you are not sure what I am saying, let me be blunt: The Divine Feminine knows that in fact, *women* are supposed to lead the world, that *only women* can change the world for the better and She wants to give women *one last chance* to step up and do so. I've come across many women that truly believe that someone else is responsible for their oppression, for the lack of opportunities in life or for the fact that they aren't leaders already. But all of it is utter nonsense. Women are responsible for the way the world is—it's just that they haven't learned to really use their powers yet to shape it the way it really can be. As a result of their lack of spiritual development, the world itself is more animalistic than divine. And in an animalistic world, women cannot succeed.

Instead of using their unique powers, many women have decided to follow the boys down the path of animalism, competing in physical ways, attempting to dominate others, even yelling and screaming on the streets, as if any of it will bring about change. But the Divine Feminine has had enough. She wants women to get serious about spirituality and become full-fledged, beautiful, powerful women.

If they fail, they will simply be *redesigned*, to no longer have the powers that they are blessed with. This will happen over a long period of time, long enough for people to not notice, but at some point, the loss of femininity will be the death of humanity.

This is why I have been asked to write this book, as well as turn my home into an Ashram of sorts for any truly committed young women to use my love and wisdom as a source for their own spiritual transformation, while sharing the details of their journey with the world so everyone can see the process unfold, something that hasn't ever been done before. Young women need to understand that their spiritual development is the *only* thing that will allow humanity to progress, and they need to see what it actually looks like instead of being given dumb narratives about what it's like to be in Divine Union, or in ecstasy, for example.

Thing is, it's possible for women to walk the spiritual path and become enlightened in a way that demolishes their femininity and become someone that is neither masculine nor feminine and both at the same time. This is what many female yoginis have done so far—they're just beyond all gender and such. This is *not* what we need in the world. We need women to remain women and see things clearly, to retain their femininity, not demolish it on the path to perfect union.

But what exactly is it that women are blessed with that allows them to change the world in a way the boys cannot? There are four specific powers, all of which come from the feminine, that I will describe. When these are put together, it allows anyone who embodies an exceptional level of Grace to make great changes to the world.

INVITATION

A woman has the power to invite or disinvite people into her world in a way that the boys simply cannot. Whether or not she realizes it, every woman creates a world around her, and everyone that she encounters in her world is someone she has invited into it, consciously or unconsciously. The problem with young women today is that they are walking around as if all the entrances to their world are wide open, all the time. This is the way that the boys are expected to walk the path of light, not the girls. To be open to the world and to give to all that come to them freely and generously is the duty of boys on this planet, not the duty of women. And even when it comes to the boys, the only thing that the boys should be giving is love, not anything else.

Instead, the boys are totally out of control, and they throw their energy around like it doesn't matter. Many girls have picked up on this idiotic practice and have started doing the same, which is nothing short of disastrous. When a woman communicates to the world that she is willing to throw her energy around, and she has all the entrances to her world open, every kind of creature that can crawls into her world and decides to hang out. Soon, a woman finds her world full of monkeys, snakes and critters of all kinds she doesn't really want (metaphorically speaking). But these animals do not listen to reason, nor are they smart enough to know what to do. They'll hang out, take what they want, defile her world and leave at some point. And women are left wondering why the hell their life is full of dumb experiences.

If you want to see a simple and clear example of what this looks like, just go to any busy coffee shop where there's a young girl manning the front counter. You'll see innumerable numbers of idiots hitting on her, trying to get a response from her, trying to get her to talk, whatever. This shouldn't ever happen to a woman, and it won't happen if the woman has her world closed off to the wrong sort. The narrative of the world may be that she is an employee at a counter in a business, but in reality, she's a woman allowing people to come into her world and receive something. When women can't see what is actually going on, they allow just about anything to happen to them. No wonder women worldwide are taken advantage of in so many ways.

If you, as a woman, are hoping for the world to grow up and change, you'll be waiting forever. It is you, as a woman, that needs to close your world to people, things and experiences you don't want. This is not a conscious power—none of the powers I am describing here are. It is an unconscious power—one that will operate on your behalf when your body starts to become intelligent and learn the way the world actually works. When it works properly, only people you want will come into your life and they will only receive what you're sharing, end of story. What this means in the world, is that if you are a woman running a coffee shop, you will literally not have idiot customers walking in. They will go elsewhere. That's how powerful it is.

Unfortunately, instead of developing this power, women are hoping that education, legislation or worse—a negative attitude—will turn away the wrong sort. This will not happen. Some women have become so jaded by their experiences that they've decided to just be unwelcoming to everyone. This is a bad idea, because of the second power women are blessed with.

RECEPTIVITY

Receptivity means that you are willing to accept life's gifts as they come to you. As a woman, you are basically a vacuum in human form, sucking up all that life is throwing at you as you go about it. Everyone, everything, everywhere is trying to give you something, which is a good thing. As a woman, you aren't expected to run around trying to make things happen, but are expected to allow things, resources, love and such be given to you so you can *create* a beautiful world out of it and then *invite* the right people, things and experiences into your world. If you stayed put in one place and worked on yourself, what you needed would walk into your life in one way or another. Instead, nowadays women are running around the world hungry for experiences.

The hunger for experience is a distinctly feminine trait, one that gets a lot of young women into trouble because they go seeking all the garbage of the world without realizing it. And of course, just about everyone is interested in giving you something, while squeezing your sweetness, your energy, your life out of you to feed their own hunger. Pretty much everyone you've ever seen exposed in the media for one reason or another is a victim of such a life—they just don't realize how damaging it is to them. By the way, if you are walking the path of light, you must avoid people who are constantly exposed to the world, whether on TV, social media, movies, etc. People who are constantly exposed to the world are not bad people, but you have no idea just how much poison these human beings carry unknowingly, thanks to the enormous amounts of negative attention they receive. The world of such people is self-contained: do not associate with it.

When your body starts to become more intelligent, you will know how to receive the right stuff, reject the rest and move on with your life. For instance, if you, as a woman, are manning the counter at a coffee shop and a boy decides to start flirting with you, you'll know how to use his energy without giving an iota of your energy back in return, then filter his energy, throw away the garbage (aka bad information), and use it to make your world a better place. Don't pity such boys, by the way—they'll learn from their stupidity one day or another.

Understand that when you go to work, your focus should be entirely on your own spiritual development, which means you *never* have to smile, wave, "be friendly," or do anything of the sort. You can just be equanimous, just do your job and nothing else. Yogis like me will give you lots of love to help you move forward when we see that you are serious about your life. We don't need you to be polite or friendly with us. In fact, when I see women throwing themselves around, it makes me nauseous.

Receptivity is also what will help you understand when life is telling you to make a change, move cities, find a new job, change your relationships, whatever. When your world is in good shape, only good things will come into it and at that point, you will happily say yes to whatever is being given to you.

As I shared with you before, the world is a projection of millions of entities, all of whose picture reels combine to create the world we see. When you, as a woman, create a beautiful world and so does your sister, the whole world eventually becomes a beautiful amalgamation of little worlds, each of which is open to some and not to others. That's how you all get to change the world, not by any other means.

But to fill your world with only the good stuff, you need the next two powers.

NAVIGATION

Most people's idea of navigation is getting from point A to point B, but this is not what I mean by navigation here. The world of spirit, i.e., the world that lies outside the realm of consciousness, does not follow the laws of existence. There is no Time there, no space, no limitation of any sort in fact. It is, therefore, a world where just about anything is possible. A subset of that is allowed in the realm of existence, and in the realm of Time, there are a few more limitations. Navigation is the ability to traverse the possibilities in the realm of the spirit and figure out how they may be manifested in the reality in which we live while fully understanding the ramifications of making those possibilities manifest. This requires the ability to envision a future that doesn't exist and then bring it to life.

If you think that a lot of people on this Earth are doing that right now, you'll be forgiven for once again giving in to worldly narratives that have reduced "envisioning" to something that just about every business leader seems to be able to do. Envisioning isn't just about taking something already here and making it slightly better or imagining a future where an existing problem is solved in a different way.

Envisioning is about doing something that literally has never been done before, not in some small way, but in a profound way that changes life on the planet fundamentally. For instance, if you can envision a world where we don't use more efficient vehicles, but eliminate transportation entirely, you'd be on the right track. This is the kind of possibility that people in general will never actually come up with, because it won't make any sense to them. Or, if you want to envision something smaller, you could envision a world where all women who have given birth have at least three years of full support to take care of their child, no matter what their life situation is. I am not talking about your "company" giving you three years "off," but about every woman on the planet having all the time she needs to care for her child, with everything she needs provided to her freely and with no strings attached.

Once you start to really envision, you'll understand that real changes don't happen by legislation, disruption or protest. They happen when you and your fellow sisters create a new world that didn't exist before and you do it in a way that takes care of all the ramifications—social, environmental and so on. This is what is missing in our world, because everyone is interested in making a small change to the way things are while ignoring many, many factors that are affected by that change. Instead, you need a universal intelligence, one that can see the big picture and then do the right thing by manifesting the right stuff. In other words, humanity needs to be patient and grow more intelligent before creating something new instead of operating with limited intelligence and making a mess. You can be sure the boys will not take the lead on this, but if you as a woman do take the lead and eventually teach your children to do the same, the future will look *very* different.

CREATIVITY

If navigation is the power you use to figure out what to manifest, creativity is the actual act of manifesting it. Once again, the world's idea of creativity and its standard for what counts as creativity is nonsensical. Creativity isn't about giving voice to your pain, sorrow and feelings, as so many musicians are doing. It isn't about putting down a description of your nightmares into scripts, as is being done in the movies. It isn't about putting your thoughts down on paper, as so many writers have done, nor is it about simply flailing around in response to whatever impulses your body may be receiving as I've seen some performance artists do. All of those are things a machine can do and with the rise of Artificial Intelligence, we will, in fact, start to see exactly these kinds of "creative acts" everywhere, because they are little more than acts of recycling the trash that is in our environment and molding it into something different. Even a machine can capture the energy and information floating around and remix it into something "new," but there's nothing creative about that. Creativity is a spiritual power, one that *literally* gives life to something that until now was only a possibility.

Women do this at a biological level all the time. They take what is not yet here—a new possibility—and give it life in the form of a child. Women don't realize that even in this situation they have the power to shape their wombs so they can invite the right kind of life into it, but we are far from that level of spiritual development on this Earth at the moment. What women can and should do though, is put their energy into giving *life* to something that was lifeless before. Whether or not something is life-giving is something you cannot measure or describe in words, but it can be experienced. For instance, most of the objects in our civilization, like furniture and cars, are lifeless because they are not actually products of creativity. In fact, many of them were made by machines! But go to a really good restaurant, and you'll see something or the other on your plate that is bursting with life (even if it's "dead"). This is part of the reason I recommend that a man cook for his family, because he can infuse everything he cooks with his life energy. When you, as a woman, receive his energy, you can create something beautiful in your world and literally give it life in a way that someone who isn't creative cannot.

It doesn't matter what you do in your life—whether you make a cup of coffee or paint a painting—once your creativity starts to bloom and you start to give life to a higher possibility instead of simply "expressing your thoughts and feelings," you'll see a whole different kind of life in what you create. And that is what the whole world needs to sustain itself.

Living creatively isn't an attitude—it happens when your body starts to function at a different level of energy than what most women live at. I can make this happen easily to any woman, but to sustain it takes a lot of work, which is why I've been asked to let women do the hard work of raising their energy while simply using my love as a source of power. Obviously, this option is only open to women who wish to live with me and go all the way to the end.

For the rest of you though, creative living is something that will happen to you if you follow the practices in this book. If you start to pay close attention to your life, a time will come when you realize that you are doing *everything* in your life in a creative manner, even brushing your teeth. It will become so natural that you will *never* want to go back to living the way you used to. Once that happens, all of life will become an incredibly meaningful act of creativity. Then, no one will need to tell you what the meaning of life is. You'll know it by living it.

TRUE POWER

True power works in total silence. Women who are exceptionally powerful tend to become quieter and quieter, because they tend to change their environment simply by showing up. It is this possibility that everyone is hoping a woman can embody, which is why whenever a woman shows up at a gathering (especially a gathering of boys), things change. People expect women to know how to navigate, which is why a woman lost in the world comes across as an idiot. People expect a woman to invite only the right people into her life, which is why no one wants to see women as victims no matter what they go through. People expect a woman to see a possibility and understand its ramifications, which is why most people expect women to say something truly amazing when they speak. People expect a woman to be life-giving wherever she goes, which is why whenever a woman shows up, everyone hopes there will be magic involved.

More than being disrespectful of women, the world is utterly *disappointed*. Women are so much more intelligent than the boys ever can be, and our young women are *super* intelligent. If they wanted to go places spiritually, they would surpass me, surpass the gurus that came so far, all the saints, even Jesus. And this is what the expectation is—that at some point women will wake up and surpass everyone who came before.

The Sanskrit word for the feminine principle of the cosmos is Shakti, which *literally* means power. This is what women are supposed to be— embodiments of true power, embodiments of the Divine Feminine.

Only women can decide if they want this for themselves.

COMMITMENT, TIMES THREE

Throughout this volume I have consistently laid out for you the way by which you can get to an experience of truth, beauty and love. Hopefully you can appreciate the fact that the narrative is mostly about *losing*, not gaining. You will lose all that is false and of no value, which includes relationships that don't matter, possessions you don't need, skills you won't use, powers you don't have but believe you do, beliefs you've been using to console and comfort yourself and many other things.

One of the things that people don't expect to lose along the path of light is hope. Unfortunately, the world has become addicted to the idea of hope, that there is a better future ahead and that it will come someday. It will not come any day, unless you're willing to give up hope and actually work for a better future. Hope is such a debilitating and destructive idea that it really causes people to act as if they are disabled in some way. Most people I've met who speak about hope are the laziest people of all—unwilling to really work hard at what matters, prioritizing instead an existence characterized by numb compliance, obedience based on fear and then layering on it all a narrative of hope and redemption that is somehow going to be theirs even if they do nothing.

On the path of light, you will totally lose hope, faith and all else that you've been holding on to. You will have to learn to live without any support whatsoever, because at the end of the day, the life you're experiencing isn't even yours!

Remember that you, the spirit, are looking through a tiny window into existence—a window called 'the human being'—and witnessing a life unfold. It is you, through inattention and wrong attention that have caused the human being to be misguided and misdirected. Once you become interested in paying attention to the right stuff, the human being you are looking through will come back into balance and live a beautiful life.

All the practices in this book, as well as spirituality in general, are about essentially helping you pay attention, because in our existence, attention is love, power, energy and all that really matters. Everyone, from the wealthiest CEOs to the poorest little high school girls, are all vying for attention, desperate for any little bit of energy, love and power that they may be able to use for their own benefit. But the only one that needs to pay attention to your life is you. And as you grow in attention span, the power that *you* bring into your life is what makes changes to it, not some "God" or even the Divine Feminine. She and other powers that exist in the universe will come to you when *you* have the power to fulfill *them*, not the other way round. In other words, you must be fierce, able to hold attention for as long as necessary on the tiniest little detail, and not be swayed by the distractions and vagaries of the world in which you currently live. And that's not for the weak.

Spirituality has always been for the few. In the past, people were told that only a few would be chosen for such an endeavor, but that time is long gone. Now, *all* of you are called, and *all* of you have been chosen. It's just a question of whether you're going to do the work, or if you're going to convince yourself that you don't have what it takes and slink back into the darkness in which you have been living all along. Still, this takes strength, strength that is *developed*, not simply given. It is developed by repeated hits, failures, setbacks and what not. Unfortunately, most people believe that persistence is something you need to succeed in the world. It is not. Persistence is what you need to succeed *in life*, but persistence must be tempered with patience, wisdom and clarity—all of which take time to come to you. You must be willing to wait when necessary. Let me give you an example from my own life to illustrate.

MY PRACTICE

Towards the end of my healing period, Sadhguru came into my life to support my work. I hadn't ever heard of him, but he suddenly appeared in my world one fine day and started to guide me. All my life I have "discovered" all kinds of meditations simply by being quiet, but this was a whole different kind of technology, so to speak. He had created something spectacular, a way for all humanity to give themselves to the spiritual process, and in the process created a sort of "bad information incinerator." I was given the ability to use his technology, to throw people as well as their garbage into the incinerator as necessary. However, that required that I operate at an incredibly high level of energy, energy I didn't have because I was totally depleted from all my past work and healing.

The practice he gave me took exactly 6 weeks to bear fruit, but in those 6 weeks, I went from zero to 100. During those 6 weeks, I got up every morning, took a shower and sat down for my practice exactly at 3:40 AM as he prescribed. I would practice *exactly* as I was taught, without a single variation of my own. I would experience total silence and bliss and then an hour later, be completely lost in a feeling of ecstasy and happiness. This feeling would last all day, carry me through my office duties and then by the time I fell asleep, I would feel like I had been *shredded* and lose all awareness of my surroundings. I didn't have any energy at night, which means my body constantly kept me awake. I usually slept less than an hour, if that.

All day I would be given spiritual insights, worldly insights or be immersed in a spiritual experience of some sort, while continuing my work at the office. It was intense, incredibly painful and full of suffering, non-stop. I would sometimes find myself shaking and shivering uncontrollably because of how little energy I had, and I was *always* cold, tired and hungry, no matter how many layers I wore or how much I ate.

My family at the time was totally unsupportive, didn't understand and didn't want to understand, which meant that I went through all of that entirely alone. For my part, I didn't have the words I have today to explain it all, which meant everyone was frustrated with the way I spoke about my experiences, all the time.

But despite all that, every morning, indeed every moment, I continued the practice. How? I literally gave myself up.

Every time I sat down for my morning practice, I visualized the guru as a funeral pyre, and I jumped into it. No matter what came out of me, I threw it into that blazing fire that was the guru. I didn't save a thing for myself, nor was I interested in survival. My commitment to the practice was absolute. As a consequence, I went from having almost no energy to having an enlightenment experience in 6 weeks.

The reason most of you will take a lifetime to complete your spiritual journey, if not more, is simply because you're not committed enough. It has nothing to do with what you possess, how much energy you have, what responsibilities you have to shoulder, etc. Sure, energy is necessary, but I am only writing this book for the ones that have it, so that's not the problem. It's just that you're not committed enough to find truth, beauty and love. Just about everything else is more important to you. You are unwilling to let your whole world fall apart to emerge into reality, unwilling to give up your cherished beliefs and you desperately long to hold on to all you have, while hoping to arrive in Heaven with all your baggage in hand.

EVERY MORNING, RECOMMIT

The ultimate practice is simple: wake up every morning and recommit to your life. Say to yourself that you will pay attention to everything, no matter how tired you are. If you fall asleep exhausted, good for you—because only when you are dead tired will you grow. Be relentless, ask yourself the hard questions and fess up to everything you've done wrong, as far as you know. You don't have to go to other people and apologize to them for hurting them, for example, (although doing that *is* the shortest path to healing from some wounds) but, on an ongoing basis, you *must* admit to yourself whatever it is you've done poorly, not done well enough or simply done wrong.

You need not keep a diary. In fact, keeping a diary is a bad idea, because it means you're keeping whatever you've thrown up in the past for you to look at periodically. You must always throw away whatever you confess, whether in writing, painting, poetry, whatever. The most effective way to confess is simply by yourself, alone and in silence. All you must do is acknowledge all that you've made a mess of, daily, weekly or even moment-by-moment and then you'll automatically move forward.

You don't even have to tell yourself that you'll do better, because that is not up to you. Many times, your sense of right and wrong will shift and you'll find that your confession was simply a question of seeing things poorly. Sometimes, you will believe you've done the wrong thing when you haven't. You will understand the truth as you go, not overnight.

But the important thing is this: act on your understanding, not on someone *else's* understanding or wisdom. If you don't walk in the direction that you believe is correct, you'll never discover if you were right or wrong. In the past, people were given specific instructions on how to live their lives because they were considered too stupid to be told the truth: that there isn't anyone else in charge of your life, nor are you in charge of it. *Life* is in charge of itself, and you must allow your life to take its course, however painful it may be to you.

SEPARATING THE SEED FROM THE CHAFF

I keep telling you how hard the spiritual path is because I don't want you to take it lightly. Unless you are willing to give it your all, I don't want you to begin. But there is another reason.

There is an upheaval coming, one that will not end the world, but one that will change civilization drastically. I was sent here to tell you that those of you who walk the path of darkness will not make it. And even among those who walk the path of light, few will survive.

I didn't come here to sell you a message of hope, to start a movement and lead the masses into some new era. I was sent here so I could say to you "look, that's the way" and point you towards a path that is barren, rocky, and going uphill for as far as the eye can see and beyond. I came here to separate the seed from the chaff. The seed will grow, while the chaff, and those who hold onto the chaff, will burn, eventually turning into ash and be used as fertilizer for future generations.

My path through this world has left a trail of destruction. This destruction is not physical, because physical destruction doesn't mean anything. The kind of destruction that terrorists, protesters and disruptors engage in only strengthens the system and deepens ignorance. No, the destruction I have left behind is spiritual—beliefs, practices, systems and even institutions are about to come crumbling down in the next few decades as this spiritual destruction begins to manifest. This is a good thing, because all that is false needs to be destroyed for it to be replaced with what is good.

How does this work? Simply put, people like me (and people like you once you advance to a certain level) are doorways to the love beyond. We are like the holes in existence that let love in, and whatever love touches turns into ash. During this process, all that is false goes first, meaning that wherever people like us go, we tend to make the falsehoods around us fall apart. All we have to do is be quiet. That's all.

STOP BEING A CHILD

Understand this clearly: the world is fine. There is nothing wrong with the world that you need to *fix*. Whatever is happening, is happening because people have designed this world the way it is. The world as it is, is simply a manifestation of the desires of people. Everyone is experiencing exactly what they wanted—they just don't realize that they wanted it. You don't have to feel pity for all the human beings that are stuck in warzones, are experiencing malnutrition, genocide, persecution, poverty, disease and death. Everyone is getting their due, one way or another. You will not be able to help them, but you certainly *can* make the world a worse place to live by interfering, which is what the masses are always up to.

If you want to create a better world, first take care of *your world*, not *the world*. And the way you take care of your world is by demolishing it completely so that a better world can be built. You don't have to *do* anything for this to happen. Just pay attention to your life and your world will fall apart in the right ways and be put back together in the right ways. Once you live in a better world and so does your neighbor, the whole world will change.

That's what it takes, not the kind of nonsense that most human beings are engaging in, where they constantly interfere and intervene in natural processes in hopes of making things better.

No matter how wonderful you think the achievements of human beings have been so far (from heart stents to space rockets), they are child's play, created by a bunch of stupid and selfish children that don't even understand who they are, much less create something of value. The mess that is the world today is a direct consequence of the immaturity with which you all have approached yourselves. This immaturity has allowed you to hide behind claims of ignorance or innocence while you destroy life but neither the universe nor the powers that be are fooled. Stupidity has caused you to invent all kinds of "needs" such as friendship, comfort, safety, security, even politics and religion—just to survive—all while less intelligent creatures such as the plants, animals and rocks continue to live harmoniously without any of them.

It is time that you all stop thinking of yourselves as children of a higher "God" who is here to take care of you in some way. It is time that you stop thinking of the Earth as your mother, depleting her by sucking at her teat, and start seeing her as your partner. It is time that you stop looking at all that humanity has created as something worth keeping and recognize what has happened so far—most of it is of no value. It is time that you accept yourselves for who you really are: the ultimate power, looking through a window into a life that you can shape through attention or destroy by inattention. It is time that you stop seeing existence as some kind of pleasure cruise. It is time that you take life seriously, get to work and create a beautiful world.

Playtime is over. It is time to grow up.

THE AUTHOR

To contact Yogi Shashi Penumarthy, email him at:
Ryll.tucson@gmail.com